THE HAPPY DEPRESSIVE

How to live, thrive and survive
with chronic depression

Steve Richards

Grosvenor House
Publishing Limited

This book is published by
Grosvenor House Publishing Ltd
Link House
140 The Broadway, Tolworth, Surrey, KT6 7HT.
www.grosvenorhousepublishing.co.uk

A CIP record for this book
is available from the British Library

ISBN 978-1-80381-860-3
eBook ISBN 978-1-80381-861-0

To Dad, who was of the generation
that didn't know how to ask for help

Contents

Apologies   vii

Today   ix

Main Characters   xi

Introduction   xiii

1 Repressed Memories   1

2 Two Voices   9

3 Surviving the Bullies   25

4 The Aftermath   33

5 Behind Every Happy Depressive....   43

6 The Pills (and more pills)   51

7 Or Not The Pills   69

8 CBT   75

9 Psychotherapy   83

10 How to Cope – While Working   89

11 How to Cope – With Retirement   101

12 Not Guilty   111

13 The Upsides   115

14 A View from Her Indoors   123

In a Nutshell   129

About the Author   135

Website Address   136

Apologies

I feel I should apologise to Alistair Campbell, the well-known spin doctor for the British Labour party during the Blair and Brown eras, for stealing his title. He also wrote a book with a similar title - *"The Happy Depressive: In Pursuit of Personal and Political Happiness"*. I didn't consciously steal it. From the moment the idea for this book first came to me I felt like The Happy Depressive was the perfect title – after all that is what I am. It was only when I was two thirds through writing, and pondering what I might put on the cover of the book, that my Googling threw up the cover of Alistair's book. So I did the obvious thing and bought it so I could read it.

It has a similarity to my book in that it isn't very long. We both say what we have to say and then stop when we are done. It doesn't take long to read and is beautifully written. Yet it is also quite a different book from mine. As you can probably tell from his subtitle, it not only deals with his own personal experience of depression (which is different from, and at certain times much more severe than, mine) but also with the thorny political issue of how to increase the happiness of the nation as a whole. I wouldn't dream of trying to tackle the latter.

It is also clear that he and I are quite different people. Though I am burdened with depression I am blessed with an optimistic and generally upbeat personality. This allows me to grasp happiness when it comes around more easily than Alistair, who really struggles but nevertheless considers himself overall to be happy.

So I decided to keep my title and express with my own subtitle the difference of approach. If you are interested in the very worthy subject of how to increase the level of happiness of a nation, I thoroughly recommend his book. If you want to know how you as an individual can achieve personal happiness despite having depression then I hope you will read mine – and I hope it helps.

Today

This morning I sat on the balcony next to my bedroom, looking over the garden with my morning cuppa. I love sitting out there when I can. It was a cool autumn day but the sun was out and the balcony caught enough of the morning sun that a thick dressing gown could ward off the chill. My wife Anne was away visiting her dad so the house was unusually quiet and empty. Though I felt her absence keenly, I could enjoy a cigarette with my tea without her telling me what I already know.

I watched the birds fly past and enjoyed the aerial acrobatics of the wood pigeons. Once again I marvelled at how graceful these voracious eaters can be in the air. There was a gentle breeze and I watched it ruffle the leaves on some of the beautiful trees around our property. I focussed on a Japanese maple with its vibrant red leaves and saw that, even in this slight breeze, several leaves were vibrating violently. I waited to see if they could all hang on for one more day. In the time taken to finish a cup of tea and a fag they all survived. I felt a strange kinship with them.

I was one week into getting acclimatised to my latest anti-depressant and it was working well. It had put an end to a tough period of insomnia and I could feel myself returning to full power.

Most of all I was, in that moment, truly happy.

Main Characters

Me: The eponymous Happy Depressive, and now Author

Anne: Beloved wife, proof-reader and essential support mechanism

Harry: A wizard of Cognitive Behavioural Therapy

Voice 1: The voice of reason a.k.a. The Real Steve

Voice 2: The voice of depression a.k.a. Mr Negativity

Voice 1:	"I'm thinking of writing a book."
Voice 2:	"And what makes you think you're up to that?"
Voice 1:	"What do you mean? I've written quite a few things."
Voice 2:	"Do you mean those silly short stories?"
Voice 1:	"Well, yes, and those articles I've written."
Voice 2:	"Anyone can write 20 pages – a whole book is another matter."
Voice 1:	"You may have a point. Still it is worth a try."
Voice 2:	"What is it about anyway?"
Voice 1:	"It is an autopathography."
Voice 2:	"Is that an autobiography of someone pathetic? Sounds about right"
Voice 1:	"No, it is an autobiographical work about dealing with an illness – in my case how to cope with depression."
Voice 2:	"B-o-ring"
Voice 1:	"You are in it."
Voice 2:	"Oh, really?"
Voice 1:	"Yes. I tell people what a pain you are and how to ignore you."
Voice 2:	"………"
Voice 1:	"What? Nothing to say to that. Are you sulking?
Voice 2:	"………"
Voice 1:	"Good. Keep quiet then. I've got a book to write."

Introduction

Do you suffer from depression, or are you close to someone who does and struggling to help them cope with the daily grind of this invisible disease? If you are, maybe you have gone online and have found a virtual mountain of books by psychologists dealing with the condition. Wouldn't it be nicer to talk to a friend? Ideally one who also lives with depression but seems to be coping pretty well. A natural storyteller, perhaps, who can share their own experiences in simple language and shed some light on how it is possible to live well despite the challenges. Maybe I can be that friend. Though we can't sit down over a cup of tea, put the kettle on, or pop a cork, and sit with my book for a while to see how it goes. If I succeed in helping just one person to live a happier life, then it was worth adding my book to that very large pile.

If we are to be friends, let's get to know each other a little better. I am not a trained therapist or counsellor, though I have always been interested in psychology and recently took a masters level course on the subject to learn more. The main thing I offer is the experience of decades of living with a mental illness that so many of us suffer from and yet so few talk about.

My depression began around 1987, when I was twenty-six years old. I know this because at the time my condition was diagnosed, my psychiatrist asked me to look back. Together we had identified the symptoms that he attributed to my depression (and the anxiety which often comes with it), and he asked me to think when those symptoms first began. I was shocked to discover, at thirty-six, that I had been struggling on in ignorance for a decade.

So my first qualification for helping you is ten years' experience of what not to do when you have depression. At the time of writing I am sixty-three, so the good news is I also have twenty-seven years' experience of learning to cope with it successfully. In the following chapters I hope to share that experience with you in an informative and entertaining way.

This is not an autobiography. It does not start at the beginning or finish at the end. Rather the book uses anecdotes and episodes from my own story to illustrate how depression can affect your quality of life, and each chapter seeks to offer ways to minimise that effect. Some of them can get quite exciting, like my adventures in the Philippines which illustrate why you should ignore your inner voice of doubt and negativity (what I call Voice 2). Others are more explanatory but are full of useful information that nobody ever tells you – such as what it is like being on anti-depressant pills for decades or what happens when you try to come off them.

Clearly my experience will not necessarily replicate yours or the experience of those you care for. My depression is long term and chronic in nature, but not as severe as many suffer. It refuses to go away, but it is manageable using the strategies I describe and with the help of medication. Many people have more severe attacks which can lead to breakdowns and hospitalisation. I would not expect my experience to offer much insight in such cases.

People with bipolar conditions, who have to navigate manic phases as well as depression, can find it much harder to find medication which stabilises them without suffering side effects as unbearable as their untreated condition. But if there are parallels between my condition and the one which interests you, then I hope that knowing you are not alone in facing this challenge brings some comfort.

For chronic sufferers like me, the first challenge is accepting that depression and anxiety may be with us for the rest of our lives. Then we can concentrate on the best way of coping with it. Life will be a mixture of good days, poor days, and the odd really bad day. If the ratio of good to bad is heavily in favour of the latter, some change in approach is needed. On the really bad days I find it is best to accept that normal functioning just isn't possible. On those days I give in and let myself hit rock bottom in order to bounce up again once the worst is over.

I once explained this philosophy, of accepting these bad days, which bore no relation to how well life was going in rational terms, to a men's group I was attending. It got a violently negative reaction from one young man in the group. He was the most physically beautiful man I had ever seen, with dark, shoulder length hair, piercing blue eyes and perfect designer stubble. Most would assume that all the good things in life would fall into this guy's lap but he was clearly severely depressed.

To him the idea of accepting his depression was lifelong was life-threatening, and he needed to believe that if you were depressed there was a solution out there, but you just hadn't found it yet. I understood where he was coming from. For him life was not worth living if it didn't improve, and I truly hope he found his way out of that dark place. I have sometimes encountered a similar attitude from counsellors and psychotherapists, who believed that if my depression had not gone then there was some undiscovered issue which therapy had yet to reveal.

I do not believe that is true in my case. I have had cognitive behavioural therapy (CBT) which is a great tool to help you intercept and manage negative thoughts but does not necessarily stop those thoughts from coming. I have had psychotherapy which was really useful in identifying patterns of behaviour which had served me well in early life but were no longer appropriate. Therapy also showed me some situations which would trigger anxiety and depression, so that I might avoid or better manage such situations. I devote chapters to both of these essential tools which have helped me enormously. Yet when the therapist and I had run out of things to discuss I still had depression and I still needed my pills.

I have given this matter a lot of thought over the years and I decided that for me, and I imagine others like me, a combination of genetic predisposition (my father also suffered though never acknowledged it), personality and the way my body reacts to external physical stimulae, particularly stress, means that depression for me is a lifetime companion. One theory is that the combination of those factors leads to a deficiency in the neurotransmitter serotonin. Not every scientist agrees with that theory, but the fact remains that if I take a drug designed to increase my serotonin levels, my depression improves to a level I find tolerable. It never goes away, but I can cope.

In fact, I have done better than cope really. I have completed a successful career operating at a high level of responsibility and work pressure, maintained a stable, loving relationship with my wife, developed many fulfilling friendships and now enjoy a financially secure retirement. Perhaps more importantly I have been, and remain, happy.

It is for this reason that I decided to write this book. If you had told me in my twenties that I had depression and that I would have it for the rest of my life, and that, however well things were going in the real world, occasionally my brain would be become convinced everything was going wrong, then I would have felt very hopeless. If you had tried to tell me that nevertheless I was going to live a full and happy life I would not have believed you. I would have been wrong.

Maybe you are that person who faces this news, or fears that your situation is like mine, and you are feeling hopeless for the future. Fear not - Happy Depressives exist and I hope you will join our ranks.

Voice 1:	"I'm struggling to know how to start."
Voice 2:	"How do these patheticographies normally start?"
Voice 1:	"I am guessing with some early childhood experiences."
Voice 2:	"So what's your problem. Bore them with some cute childhood stories?"
Voice 1:	"I can't. I don't remember any."
Voice 2:	"Some writer you are. I did warn you. So make some up."
Voice 1:	"No. Though I was tempted to do that to get the therapists off my case."
Voice 2:	"They were convinced you were nuts because somebody abused you."
Voice 1:	"They were, but my childhood was just happily uneventful ."
Voice 2:	"You mean boring. Like this book is going to be by the sound of it."
Voice 1:	"That's it. Now I know how to start the book"
Voice 2:	"By telling them not to bother because it's boring?"
Voice 1:	"No dickhead, by telling them not to worry if they can't remember."

1

Repressed Memories?

"I find it very hard to remember anything about my early childhood – I think the first clear memories date from about the age of 10."

As soon as these words had left my mouth, I knew what I had let myself in for. The woman sitting opposite me, who was normally so passive, suddenly looked very alert and interested. She was a psychotherapist, from the psychodynamic school, so repressed childhood memories were her stock in trade. She was convinced she was on to something here. My heart sank a little as I knew that, for a few sessions at least, she was going to try and unearth these "blocked" memories.

She was of course just doing her job. Releasing repressed memories are a key element of psychoanalysis and many people suffering from depression in later life do find a link to early life experiences. I was certainly depressed and I did have trouble remembering my early life. Before the age of ten I only had recall of a few childhood incidents, and even then I may just have formed the memories from the number of times adults told me about them. So it was right that we spent some time investigating why I couldn't remember, even if I wasn't very keen. I am not sure if I was frightened that she would unearth something horrible or just irritated that we might be wasting time before we got to the crux of the matter.

Sitting in that therapist chair I was giving it my best shot to answer her questions about my early childhood, just in case this was indeed part of the road to recovery. We spent quite a few sessions on this, and I swear I was making a genuine effort. Yet, in the end, we both concluded that I couldn't remember my early years because they were uneventful. I had a safe, loving home environment with two parents, one younger brother and many aunties and uncles and there were no dark secrets to uncover. If only I had realised at the time that this lack of detail was going to seriously hamper my attempts at writing an autobiographical work, I might have tried harder to develop a bit of false memory syndrome.

If you have similar blanks in your childhood memories then don't let this put you off going to a therapist. It does not necessarily mean there is something horrible buried in your past. Try to find the courage to explore them with a therapist and see what kind of feelings are generated. For some these feelings will be strong and scary, suggesting that there is something to be unlocked, and there will be much work to be done in therapy to heal the underlying trauma. If, like me, it just generates mild frustration that you cannot remember anything, the chances are there is not much to remember. Sometimes people have nice but boring childhoods and sometimes those people get depression.

The issue of potentially repressed memories was to surface again later in life. In my sixties I was still suffering from depression. It was largely under control but the most annoying side effect of the drugs I was taking – interference with my sex life - was getting worse with age. I decided I was going to try and address this and I chose to do it through hypnotherapy.

The therapist sitting opposite me this time did claim to be able to help me with my sexual problem (without seeming that comfortable talking about it) but she was more interested in trying to address the underlying depression. If, she argued, we could remove or reduce that to the point where I no longer needed the pills, then the sexual problem would go away. I was not convinced. This game was now going to be played for much higher stakes than I had bargained for. If I got my hopes up for a cure and it didn't work, then I was going to feel worse. Still, the lure proved too strong and that is what we agreed to try. I don't think we ever spoke about sex again, to her immense relief.

My hypnotherapy journey started with exercises to see if I could reach a state of hyper relaxation in which my conscious mind was distracted by visualising something. This allowed the therapist, she believed, to interrogate my unconscious mind.

I proved to be very good at becoming hyper relaxed, which was nice and did bring some immediate benefits to my mood. I remember driving home from one of the sessions and getting snarled up in some bad traffic which was making me late for my next appointment. I usually do not deal very well with being late, and would normally get quite stressed about it. On this occasion I remained completely calm. I could even achieve this relaxed state at home using a recording that she provided. I would recommend learning these techniques if you too have difficulties relaxing.

Nor was I as poor at visualising as I had feared I might be. I could conjure up the mental images that she was asking me to see quite vividly. She pronounced me a good subject and the work really began. She and my subconscious were about to get acquainted.

Well, that is what she said was happening. Maybe I am too good at multi-tasking, but my conscious mind seemed quite capable of maintaining the visualisation while eavesdropping on their conversation. Which seemed to be taking a rather familiar turn.

In our early conversations I explained the conclusions I had drawn from psychotherapy and self-analysis. Due to bullying at school I developed anxiety about how other people see me. This had led me to develop a hard shell and to avoid showing any signs of weakness to others. Keeping up this superhuman exterior was quite draining and through therapy I learned to show a more human side, particularly in work situations. This had the added benefit of making me more likeable and popular. Though I believed I was a much healthier individual than before, and suffered much less with my depression, every time I tried to stop the anti-depressants I relapsed. I had come to accept that I might now just have a physical imbalance which I needed the pills to correct.

She accepted all this as a very logical conclusion for my conscious mind to come to but questioned why I was so sure the bullying was the beginning of the problem. In order for the bullying to have hit me so hard, she believed that I must already have been questioning my self worth. She was probing to find the first moment in my life at which my subconscious mind "mislearned" or misinterpreted some event to make me feel unworthy. Of course I had no conscious memory of this so she believed only my subconscious was going to provide the answers. So once again I was being led towards filling in those blanks from childhood.

While I was in a relaxed state and supposedly distracted by my visualisations she posed questions and I answered her questions with a "yes" or "no" by lifting the index finger on either my right or left hand. This method was better for allowing my subconscious mind to answer than if I had answered verbally. This bit was really hard. I was trying not to engage with the questions and to answer as automatically as possible with my fingers. Some of the questions were hard to give yes or no answers to and I felt that sometimes the finger movements got a bit random.

At the end of the question-and-answer session she was convinced that something had happened around the age of four. She put me back into the deep relaxed state and I attempted to visualise what had happened. This did conjure up a scenario in which four-year-old me was standing surrounded by towering adult figures who were berating me for being scared. They were telling me I was too old to behave like this. Though I am convinced this never actually happened it did feel emotionally very real. I was prone at that age to getting scared in bed at night and coming down for my parents to comfort me. It is possible that one time they reacted badly to me doing this and I internalised a feeling of humiliation. To be honest I don't know, and I am not sure it matters.

My hypnotherapist was delighted with this progress and finished the session by talking as if I was going to feel radically different as a result of this discovery. Sadly, however, I didn't feel any different. Then I started to feel more depressed as it seemed that this potential route to a cure was coming to nought. I even felt a bit of a failure for being bad at hypnotherapy (or at least Voice 2 was telling me it was somehow my fault).

At the next session I told her that I felt worse and she apologised for raising my expectations prematurely. However her conclusion was that in order to unblock my depression we needed to seek an even earlier event which was the real start of my problems. I began to feel like I would be back in the womb before she gave up. After that session I stopped going. My depression was no worse, my sexual function was no better but at least I now knew how to get deeply relaxed.

I want to stress that I am far from being anti-therapy. The psychotherapy helped me a lot and I know hypnotherapy works for a lot of people. (It seems very effective at giving up smoking for example.) It is just that both forms of therapy come with a health warning. Therapists engage in their particular form of therapy because they believe it works and if they come across a therapy resistant condition, or a red flag like potentially repressed memories, they often become convinced that more therapy is the answer. In some cases it will be. In others a point can be reached where the benefits of therapy have been achieved and it is time to move on. We as the clients have a role to play in deciding when that time is reached and need the confidence to do so.

Voice 1:	"So we are coming to the part where you have a starring role."
Voice 2:	"Tell me why I should care?"
Voice 1:	"Don't you always think you are in the right?"
Voice 2:	"I don't think it, I know it."
Voice 1:	"Then I thought you would be glad of the attention."
Voice 2:	"But that is exactly your problem."
Voice 1:	"What is?"
Voice 2:	"You don't pay attention to me?"
Voice 1:	"True."
Voice 2:	"You are just as foolhardy as you have always been."
Voice 1:	"Yes. Because what you call foolhardy, I call fun."

2

Two Voices

It was my first job out of college, working in a design office in the thriving metropolis of Sidcup in Kent, and I was already bored. My first task was to design some reinforced concrete beams for a power station in Paraguay. The first time I did this I was quite excited as it was much more practical and real than anything I did at college. Within days of me finishing the design and signing off the drawings, real people in Paraguay were going to be building that beam. The two hundredth time I did that, six months later, the excitement had waned – and there were still many beams to go.

Sitting at my desk, with my Concrete Designers Handbook open, and trying to build up enthusiasm for beam number 201, I got a slightly ominous call. It was from the MD's secretary and he wanted to see me straight away.

I went up to his office on the top floor and found him with one of the directors and they asked me to take a seat.

"How are things going Steve?" asked the MD. "Are you settling in OK?

"Yes thank you sir. Beavering away on the Paraguay substations."

"Excellent, excellent. You ever done any surveying?"

I had the feeling that the right answer was yes. It wasn't a total lie – I had done a two-week surveying field trip at university. We mainly got drunk and terrorised the locals. One night the rugby boys decided to raid the girls' dorm and scare a load of botanists half to death, and nearly got sent home. In the day we did learn the basics of how to use a level and a theodolite so that counts surely?

So I said, "Yes sir. Why?"

"Daniel here is running our Philippines Mini-Hydro project and we need someone to go out for three months and do a spot of surveying for the feasibility stage. You up for that?"

"Definitely, sir."

"OK, he will fill you in. You will need to leave next Monday. Have a great time."

I knew the right answer was yes. Voice 1 had told me so.

Later that day voice 2 woke up.

"Surveying? What do you know about surveying?

"Why didn't you tell them you only had two weeks mucking about in the Buckinghamshire countryside?"

Voice 1 had the answer. "Because then they wouldn't have sent me."

"Exactly, they would have sent somebody who knew what they were doing, not someone who is going to screw up. In the Philippines of all places – you have never been further than Spain and then you were freaked out because they didn't speak English."

"I expect they will have translators."

"You know even less about hydro power – what is a mini hydro anyway? Richards you are a damn fool."

I was twenty-one – only six months out of university. It was about five years before I consider my depression really started, yet I was already familiar with the two voices in my head. Not truly voices of course, more streams of thought, but streams which seemed to come from two entirely different people. Voice 1, who I later came to think of as the real me, was rational and confident. He knew that I was clever and adaptable, that I had rarely failed at anything I tried, and he was bored and craved adventure. Voice 2, who I later came to view as the voice of depression, was Mr Negative. He was the stoker of my fear of failure and delighted in telling me how many ways that failure might come. Learning how to manage these two voices would become key to my survival as a happy depressive. So in my case of the job in the Philippines let's see who was right.

The first thing I needed to do was break it to my then girlfriend (now wife) that in less than a week I was going away for three months. I told her in Safeways and she claims that we were halfway through the weekly shop when I casually said

"Oh, by the way, I have to go the Philippines for three months."

"What? When?"

"Next Monday."

She thought I was joking. She still teases me about this today.

A week later I was flying Club Class on Cathay Pacific to Manila. (This distorted my idea of what air travel was like for years to come. I had only ever been on one package holiday flight to Spain before this. Now I was reclining in my own private berth on a plane and being served delicious food with real cutlery. It was a long time before I got that treatment again.)

We had a three-hour stopover in Hong Kong and this is where Voice 2 scored his first points. As I left the cabin to walk down the steps to the bus I almost took a step back in shock. I remember feeling like someone had turned on a powerful hairdryer and aimed it up my trouser legs as the heat and humidity hit me. I managed to recover without stepping on any toes and walked down to the airconditioned bus, by which time I had a film of sweat all over my body.

"So you are going to spend three months outside surveying in this heat eh? Good luck boyo."

By the time we reached Manila it was late and I was braced for the temperatures so it was less of a shock, but Voice 2 was chuckling away and telling me how unprepared I was. He would have a few more victories over the coming three months. The first of which came on my second night.

I had arrived about 1 am and tried to go to sleep but for me it was about 9 in the morning and there was no way I could persuade my body to sleep. I reported to the office the next day highly jet-lagged and met my new boss, Vernon. He was very short, with a bald head and a bushy beard and was almost as wide as he was tall. He was an enthusiastic rugby player who was hooker for the expat team in Manila. I had experienced the Welsh version of the rugby boys at home, with a very working-class machismo I found intimidating. At college I had met the English version – just as intimidating but posh with it. Vernon was a prime example of the latter, and I immediately knew I could not confide my uncertainty about my surveying skills to this guy.

"He is going to eat you for breakfast," Voice 2 gloated.

At the end of the working day, when all I wanted to do was collapse into bed, Vernon announced that he and the rest of the team were going to show me around Manila. I dutifully changed and met the others outside my hotel in the relatively quiet business district of Makati. They took me to a few local bars then we took a taxi to another district where the "girlie bars" were located.

As soon we left the taxi scantily clad young women were calling "Hey Joe, want some company" at us and trying to drag us into their bar. Vernon clearly had a particular destination in mind so we fought our way through and made it to the one he had chosen. Within minutes we were sat at the bar while women wearing even less crowded around us and sat on our laps while those wearing nothing at all danced above us. I was terrified. I tried not to put my hands anywhere too rude while I longed for my bed.

"You are well out of your depth, boyo," said a familiar voice.

It was well over a month before I dared to leave my hotel at night (though it turns out that with practice and exposure you can get used to semi-naked women sitting on your lap).

His next victory came after our first trip into Northern Luzon. Outside of the urban areas most of the Philippines was made up of flatlands, with a patchwork quilt of paddy fields, and hills covered in light jungle. It was not how most westerners picture jungle, which is more accurately rainforest, but a drier tangle of slender trees and bamboo which is quite difficult to penetrate once off the many logging trails used to transport timber.

We were checking out a potential site for a mini-hydro station and Vernon led us on a 13km route march up the mountain to the proposed dam site. We had to hack our way through the bamboo to find the site and then made our way back down the river to where the power station and turbines would be located. I was young and relatively fit but not used to that climate.

That night back in the hotel I started to get terrible stomach cramps and a headache from hell and had to call the hotel doctor. He told me I was severely dehydrated and that it was not enough to drink a lot on such trips but I also needed to take in enough salt to replace what was lost during perspiration. I spent two days in bed drinking litres of rehydration fluids (a disgusting salty mix of essential minerals) before I could return to work.

"Ha – I told you in Hong Kong you were not up to this you wimp. What are you going to be like when you have to do a survey as well as climb a mountain?" The answer, it turned out, was pretty rubbish.

Vernon introduced me to the equipment I was to use in my surveys. It was a very fancy piece of kit which not only measured differences in height (or level as we called it) but also distances and angles (the measurements made by a theodolite). He demonstrated how it works and it did not seem a world apart from instruments I had used at college so my confidence rose a little.

When it was time to go back to site and do the survey I travelled up alone with my driver, Pedro, by Land Rover. We stopped by the local electricity co-op to pick up my crew, then went on to Jaen, where the station would be built. Using my combined level/theodolite I made a "traverse" – i.e. we made our way up the mountain path measuring the increases in height from our starting point and the direction we were travelling in. When we got to the path through the bamboo we used our machetes (called "bolos" in the Filipino language Tagalog) to try and widen the track as much as we could so we could make sightings through the instrument, which we had to set up hundreds of times on its tripod. Once we reached the dam site on the river we turned and traversed down the river – jumping from rock to rock and setting up wherever we could find a flat surface. Eventually, in near darkness, we got back to our starting point and took the final reading.

I quite enjoyed this survey. It was hard work but I was enthralled by the scenery – though my western eyes could not pick out the wildlife that was all around us. Every hundred metres one of my crew would stop to point out a snake that I could not differentiate from the undergrowth, or a troop of monkeys hanging in the trees that I looked right through until one of them moved.

Once back in Manila I started to process my readings. The way it should work is that you start at level 0.0, work your way up the mountain calculating how much higher each reading takes you, until you get a reading for the level (or altitude) of the dam site. Then you process the readings on the way down and slowly decrease in level until you reach your starting point where, if you have done things correctly, you should arrive back at zero within a certain error range, normally a few centimetres. My error was 2 metres. My incompetence at surveying was there for all to see and however many times I checked my figures the outcome was the same.

I nervously showed these results to Vernon, who raised his eyebrows and then told me to fetch the instrument and meet him outside. We set up the tripod and he went up to it and tried to move the instrument. It moved through several degrees.

"How often did you tighten this on the way round?" he said.

"How do you tighten it?" I asked.

"You use these screws here. On a normal survey if they are tight at the beginning they will probably stay tight till you have finished. When your Filipino helper is dragging it up a mountain and you are setting up on a clump of bamboo or a rock in the river things tend to get loose so you really need to check it is tight before you take a reading."

Voice 2 said nothing, he was laughing too hard. I was expecting the bollocking to end all bollockings as my ears burned with embarrassment.

Vernon just smiled. "Luckily for you an accuracy of plus or minus one metre is good enough for a feasibility study so write it up and next time you go out use a fucking screwdriver." He never mentioned it again – and went up in my estimation from that day onwards.

So was it a five-nil victory for Voice 2 and proof that I should never have gone? Was it hell. For three months he was drowned out by Voice 1 crowing about the fun I was having, which kept me supplied with dinner party stories for many years to come. Did I experience a few moments of doubt and the odd depressed morning when I felt out of my depth? Sure. But it was worth it.

I had so many wonderful adventures in that three months that I could fill this whole book with them, but that is not really the point of the Happy Depressive. Let me just give you one example to show how right Voice 1, the real Steve, proved to be – and why you shouldn't listen to Voice 2.

The first site at Jaen was selected by someone else. The next one was down to me to find. The process we used was to start with contour maps to find rivers with potential for a mini-hydro project – defined as a hydro power station with less than 20MW capacity. We were looking for a river with flow all year round, that would have water even in the dry summer months, and which had enough "head" – the difference in height between the power station and the dam – to generate sufficient power. After pouring over the maps for about a week I found three possible sites. The next task was to visit each site and measure the flow in the river.

The three sites were spread over the north of the main island of Luzon, a large land mass (five times the size of Wales) which included the capital Manila. Given the distances to cover the most efficient way to reach them all was by helicopter. So we hired a two-seat helicopter to track them down. I flew in a terrifyingly small prop plane to the northern airport of Tuguegarao to meet up with the pilot, a smooth little guy called Tigi. We then navigated our way to the three sites and tried to land as close as possible to my selected dam sites.

Once at the site I would jump out of the chopper, climb down to the river and take a reading using a flowmeter. We also checked out the feasibility of reaching the station site by road, as we would one day need to return by Land Rover to complete the survey. Every time, within a few minutes of landing, local villagers, mainly kids, would appear from nowhere and cheer us on, so I started to take a pocketful of sweets with me. At one site the chief of police came out to greet us and invited me to stay with him when we returned.

One of the sites which proved to have enough water was up-river from an existing power station we had already designed. This one was a "Dendro" power station – a wood burning station – that relied on the accompanying plantation of fast-growing Ipil-Ipil trees for fuel. After getting clearance from head office, Pedro and I returned in our Land Rover to do the survey. We spent the night, with our crew, in the station accommodation, hosted by Jim - an English engineer overseeing the works. The next day we set off up a logging trail to a point level with the dam, then attempted to cut a route through the forest using our bolos, with me on the compass trying to guide us down to the river. Unfortunately the vegetation proved to be too thick, and we had to abandon our attempt.

Back at the station I pondered whether we had to exclude this site due to poor access, while we sat around a campfire drinking the local gin. As we sat there some men appeared through the trees and joined us around the fire. We had a great time and when they left Jim told me that they were guerrilla fighters who were hiding out in the hills and engaged in a war of resistance with the Marcos regime. They seemed to have no beef with us.

I was loath to give up on this site as it would be feasible, with appropriate machinery, to clear a route to the river from the logging trail. We could build the dam if only I could complete the survey to establish the feasibility of the site. I came up with a plan.

The next morning I told the crew we would be going up the river to find the dam site. Jim and I had arranged a special treat, or so we thought, for the men and me. A full English breakfast using Jim's supplies. I wolfed down my bacon and eggs while my crew politely ate this strange food. Soon after we loaded up our gear and set off.

Initially the terrain was similar to Jaen, and we could jump from rock to rock along the riverbed and made good progress. After about an hour the men started to complain. They usually started the day with a mountain of rice, and without it they seemed to have no energy. By now I had fully acclimatised to the heat and was usually several strides ahead of my crew, but they were falling further behind. So we had to stop and let them fill their confused bellies with rice we had packed for lunch before they would carry on.

Not long after this unscheduled stop we rounded a bend to find ourselves in a canyon. Smooth walls of rock rose ten metres on either side and the river ran slow and deep in between. No banks, and no rocks to jump between. I think the men thought "OK, now the dumb white guy will have to take us home". I was not for giving up and decided we would swim. We made a raft from wood alongside the river and balanced our equipment and most of our clothes on this raft. Then we swam, pushing this raft in front of us, through the canyon. Towards the end we passed two little boys fishing. I was told they were fishing for conga eels as the river was full of them.

The canyon rounded another bend and we could see rocks ahead which might let us proceed on land, only to notice another obstacle in our path further on – a 15m high waterfall. We climbed out and assessed the situation. There was no way around as the smooth canyon walls still ran close to the river on either side. Hopes rose again amongst the men for an early return but I remembered that we had brought a rope with us in case we needed to climb. I sent one of the guys up the waterfall, which he climbed like it was a ladder, carrying the rope. He tied it off on a tree at the top and threw the rope down. It was just about reachable from the rocks we were standing on at the bottom.

I attempted the climb next. If I couldn't get up it was pointless the others trying. For a while I made good progress, holding the wet and slippery rope in both hands, finding a foothold and then levering myself up as the water flowed over me. Then I reached a point where the available foothold was very small and I took one hand off the rope to try and pull myself up by grabbing a jutting rock with my other hand. As I pushed off my foot slipped, I lost grip on the rope and started to fall. I was maybe 8 metres up and knew that there were jagged rocks at the foot of the waterfall that would not make a good landing spot. I pushed out hard with both hands and feet and managed to throw myself clear and land in the pool below. As I sunk down I thought of conga eels and my skin crawled as I had a sudden conviction that one was about to bite me.

I surfaced, swam to the edge of the pool and climbed out. I had banged my knee but was not badly injured. I looked back up at the rope and decided not to risk another attempt. Sadly this site was going to be crossed off my list.

I wrote up my report on this visit to explain why the site was rejected and gave a full account of this adventure. Much later, when I returned to the UK, I discovered that this report had made it into the company magazine as proof of the lengths to which Balfour Beatty engineers would go in order to find suitable projects. I have relayed this story many times, often after a few glasses of wine. I always tell it with a smile on my face – and watch the faces of my audience wonder if such an outlandish story can really be true.

Pedro, Tigi and I had many more adventures, not all of them suitable to print, including the night I did get to stay with the Chief of Police. If I had my time over again I would make the same decision when the MD asked, "Are you up for that?".

We all have some version of the two voices I think, and in a relatively healthy mind the negative voice can be overcome. The rewards for doing so can be great, as I have shown. In the depressed mind however Voice 2 can drown out Voice 1 completely and become the dominant one. We start to believe these negative scenarios it describes are real, and start to make decisions on that basis. Then things get dangerous. The secret to surviving when that happens is threefold.

Firstly, if you have your pills and they work for you, then take them to give yourself a chance.

This won't silence the depressive voice completely, but it will slow down the rate at which negative thoughts arise on all but the worst days. If it is not pills that you use (more on this later), apply whatever calming technique works for you to give you that thinking time.

Secondly learn to recognise that it is the wrong voice talking and take as little notice as you can. Use whatever means you can to distract yourself and do not base any decisions on what that voice is telling you.

Thirdly don't get depressed about being depressed. The natural tendency is to look for reasons why you are depressed. To look for things in your life that may be causing it. Other people will tempt you down that path by asking you why you are depressed. Voice 2 will definitely be making unhelpful suggestions. If you look hard enough you will find something credible to blame, and then maybe make life changes in an attempt to feel better. If you are like me that won't work and you can disappear down a rabbit hole of increasing desperation trying to find the solution.

I will come back to ways to cope on a daily basis in this battle of the voices, and cover two critical tools I use every day that I learned through therapy. I needed that help and you may too. First I want to tell you about a very tough time in my life that gave Voice 2 much of his power.

Voice 1:	"Shit. The next chapter is going to be hard to write."
Voice 2:	"Because you are crap at writing?"
Voice 1:	"No, because I am going to deal with the bullying at school."
Voice 2:	"If you ask me those guys knew what they were talking about. What a wimp."
Voice 1:	"Piss off. I nearly didn't make it through those years you know."
Voice 2:	"You are not going to cry are you? I hate it when you do that."
Voice 1:	"You know I can't cry. Too well trained for that."
Voice 2:	"Well, get all sorry for yourself then."
Voice 1:	"No. I am sad for old me but happy for new me, and I want to write about it ."
Voice 2:	"Yes, but will anybody want to read it?."
Voice 1:	"We will see, won't we? But yes I think so."
Voice 2:	"For God's sake why?"
Voice 1:	"Because bullies like you get everywhere, and people need to know you can be survived."

3

Surviving the Bullies

It started, as these things often do, with something very small – a haircut. Admittedly it was a terrible haircut, the worst I have ever had, but it certainly didn't deserve the reaction it got. A reaction which I only just managed to survive.

From the ages of eleven to thirteen I was a very easy-going boy. I was not so tall and a little chubby but really didn't waste any time worrying about what I looked like or what I wore. I just got on with being me, and I assumed everybody else thought I was OK. God how I miss that boy.

At that age I wore the clothes that Mum decided I was going to wear and when she decided I needed a haircut she took me to Tom Martin's barber shop. Tom was a nice old guy with a huge walrus moustache who knew his way around a "short-back-and sides". Until the age of thirteen this is what Mum asked for and, as long as the hair was out of my eyes, I didn't care what he did. In the Autumn of 1974 she seemingly got bored with the usual and asked for something different.

I sat in the chair oblivious to this change of plan while Tom fashioned the only other style he knew, the Basin Cut. It is so called as you end up looking like someone put a basin over your head and cut around the edge. I had a fringe and from the top of my head my hair came down straight in all directions but curled under at the ends in a look reminiscent of Mary Quant. Tom and Mum seemed quite happy with this. I thought it looked pretty bad, but the hair was out of my eyes, so I just looked forward to messing it up. I went to school the next day completely unaware of the danger looming.

As I entered the classroom for registration I noticed a few suppressed giggles and the odd pointed finger, so I sensed that my new look was not going unnoticed.

Then Matthew entered, took one look at me and roared with laughter. "What the hell do you call that Richards?" he said as he pointed to my hair.

I just blushed and tried to smile but I was not enjoying this new feeling that everyone was watching me.

The ribbing continued throughout the day and Matthew started to call me Pink Perm. He was really enjoying picking on me. I pointed out that my hair was neither pink nor curly but he clearly loved the alliteration and unfortunately, as the term wore on, the nickname became popular with others too. Though he remained the ringleader, once others saw him get away with it they felt safe to join in too. By the end of that school year, long after my haircut had grown out, I was fully established as one of the uncool crowd that others looked down upon. I could not understand why this had happened.

People often speculate on why bullies become bullies, and Matthew did not seem your typical candidate as he was far from being one of the cool crowd himself. He was tall, dark, very overweight, unattractive, and crap at sports. He was a very talented artist, which I admired, but that doesn't make you cool at thirteen. He mainly gained acceptance by being witty. His closest friend was Dean who was short, blond, unattractive and crap at sports. They walked around acting the fool, like schoolboy versions of Laurel and Hardy, and I always found them both very amusing. Humour is often used to hide insecurity and to avoid getting bullied for one's physical shortcomings. They suffered a few jibes but on the whole successfully avoided the role of outcasts. That same insecurity however can make opportunities to exert power over others very attractive and kids do seem to pounce on signs of weakness. The Pink Perm stuff was clearly hurting me and sadly my reaction was encouraging Matthew to keep it going.

At the time I was not into finding psychological explanations for his behaviour. The fact that many others were now joining in and expressing negative opinions on me had an enormous impact. If everyone is picking on me, I thought, there must actually be something wrong with me. The carefree boy was gone. I became obsessed with how I looked and how to avoid inviting further derision. Tom Martin never saw me again as I demanded to go to a proper hair salon and have what I considered a more modern cut. I wore my hair long, as was the fashion, but my hair is naturally wavy and if anything I ended up fitting my nickname better. I also started carefully selecting my own clothes, within the budget Mum allowed, in an effort to blend in and become invisible again.

That third year of secondary school was no fun and I longed for the summer holidays to begin. As well as feeling fed up and nervous, I was always tired and hungry as my body had decided to put on a growth spurt. At the start of my Pink Perm days I was five foot three and a year later I was six foot, without putting on much weight whatever I ate. I was now a walking skeleton with a mop of wavy hair and a face that was handsome but could be called pretty if you wanted to undermine my masculinity. It appeared many people did.

In my town the fourth, fifth and sixth years of secondary school were at a separate campus so my tormentors and I all moved and I started year four praying for a fresh start. It was not to be.

Though the Pink Perm name had lost its impact, and was rarely used, the bullying intensified, now focussed on suggesting that I was less than a man. I was weedy (true), too sensitive, probably gay and a wimp. At my comprehensive school those at the top of the hierarchy were the hardest boys who could beat up anyone else. To underline my lowly status people would hand me lists. In one the class was ranked from the toughest at the top to the weakest at the bottom. I of course was at the bottom, below even those who I would have classed as wimps. Another list showed me at the top but stated that anyone wishing to move up the list had to beat up the one above them – implying that all the brutes and rugby boys below me would be coming to get me.

Looking back, I can see that the bullying was not that bad, and many people will have suffered worse, but the effect on me was devastating. With hormones raging, my body changing in ways I did not like, and the daily input of negative messages my self-image went through the floor. I was never going to have friends (not true even then), never find a girl and never be happy.

I got beaten up twice that year, not by my regular bullies just by random hard nuts who took a dislike to my pretty face. I gently broached the subject of bullies with my dad, without letting on I was a victim. It turned out he was officially the school bully who gave kids a beating before they moved to the upper school. He regaled me with tales of how he was once pounced on by a group of lads and badly beaten. He tracked down each one, got them alone and gave them a worse beating in revenge. His dad was really proud of him for that. So is that what real men do? Clearly, the kids at school were right and I was never going to be one of them.

I soon began to feel afraid wherever I was: at school; walking home alone at night; going to the youth club. I couldn't sleep, had a constant pain in my stomach and felt completely hopeless. I wanted it to end and started thinking about how to end it.

It is strange how thoughts of suicide can be comforting but when you can see no other option then any way for your pain to end can be quite relaxing. Luckily the means I devised for killing myself were so impractical they would not have worked even if I had tried. Without access to pills or alcohol I tried to work out how to drown myself in the bath. I even got as far as doing a few mock-ups to see how to hold my head down as I started to drown. The engineer in me was starting to emerge even then.

I spent about two months wanting to die and thinking about how that might happen when I started to tap into a pool of stubbornness that probably saved my life. I started to get angry at my tormentors and a determination grew not to let them win. They were, I decided, people with a small-town mentality and a better way to rid myself of them was to leave my small town.

I had previously been a lacklustre student. The carefree boy hadn't worried about results or the odd "must try harder" on the report card. Now I saw exams as a way to escape and I threw myself into my schoolwork. The change was dramatic and I enjoyed academic success for the rest of my life. I doubt this would have happened without the bullying, so ironically I owe much of my later achievements to this unhappy period.

At school the bullying continued for a while, but my escape plan stopped me getting desperate again. One day Matthew was being really verbally abusive and I broke down in tears. Not the way my dad, or most adults, would recommend dealing with bullies but strangely it worked. He was shocked at my reaction and I somehow reached the decent boy inside him. From that day on he never picked on me again. It had stopped being fun for him. Soon others got bored and moved on to other things and I was left alone.

Like most school bullying it lasted for a while and then it ended, and life carried on. I don't think I learned any great lessons about how to deal with bullies. You can try crying but that won't work with everyone. If you know a child going through it try to convince them that it is a short-term problem, which is nothing to do with their failings but the insecurities of others. Even those who pile on once the main perpetrator starts are probably just grateful it is not them being picked on. This may not console them – at the time it feels like life is not worth living and it will always be that way. Hopefully they will find a way to cope, as I did. However, there lies the second danger.

For me the crisis was over but the aftermath remained. This period of my life and the way I chose to cope with it, which worked at the time, was to affect my life for many years to come – and not always in a positive way. It is important not to hold on to outdated strategies once they become unhealthy.

Voice 2:	"I enjoyed that one."
Voice 1:	"I thought you might."
Voice 2:	"It reminded me of the days when you still listened to me."
Voice 1:	"Stupidly. I thought you were right."
Voice 2:	"I was. Don't show any weakness or the bullies will be back."
Voice 1:	"No. That was just fear talking."
Voice 2:	"It's right to be scared if you are weak."
Voice 1:	"I am not weak, and nobody was coming after me this time ."
Voice 2:	"Believe that if you must."
Voice 1:	"I kept up those defences for far too long"
Voice 2:	"And now you are vulnerable."
Voice 1:	"No, now I am free."

4

The Aftermath

It may seem strange to some but I do not consider the increasingly sad period around the ages of thirteen to fourteen, or the brief suicidal period which followed, as part of my depression. This is primarily because I think of my depression, or its most annoying aspect at least, as causing incredibly negative moods which do not relate to how well life is going in reality. In some ways my reaction to being bullied and struggling with puberty was a rational one. Lots of young men have suicidal thoughts at that age and sadly many of those do take their own lives. I am quite proud of the fact that I dug myself out of that hole, despite feeling that there was no one I could talk to. Nevertheless it was instrumental in causing my later problems.

Not all of the coping strategies I developed were innately unhealthy, but some were and some I hung onto for too long.

The key element of the escape plan – the academic effort and resulting success – served me very well. From a fairly low starting point I amassed ten O-Levels (GCSEs in today's jargon) three A-levels and a BSc in Civil Engineering. I have never failed any exam and academic success became a core part of my self-image. The drivers of this success were a bit negative, however. Initially it was the desire to leave my small town and the bullies behind, which morphed into a fear of failing. Being bright had started to bring me some status and I was terrified of losing it. Sometimes I would study so hard at university I would forget to eat. I had a fierce level of concentration and could produce work very quickly but I was definitely developing a perfectionist streak that would come back to bite me later.

More obviously unhealthy was that I withdrew from the world of men. It was other boys who tormented me for just being a little bit different and somehow unmanly in their eyes. I had also tried to confide in boys I considered true friends about a couple of things bothering me during puberty. (I had nocturnal emissions known as wet dreams, which was normal, but mine were very painful, and I had painful nipples during my growth spurt.) Instead of offering sympathy or advice they just ridiculed me. So I wrote off the whole male sex as being untrustworthy and vowed never to show them any weakness that would allow them to look down on me again.

I didn't withdraw physically. I still played football most nights with the lads and drank as many pints as they did in the pub. We played three card brag in the lunchtimes but emotionally I kept my cards close to my chest, and never risked sharing personal issues with them again.

I kept this up for many years. I didn't lack male friends but always maintained that emotional distance. Most of them probably never noticed or were doing the same. Occasionally I got the feeling that my reserve was affecting the closeness of the relationship, or a few times wondered if a particular friend might be looking for a deeper connection. Yet I never made the leap to opening up, and I don't have a male friend to this day with whom I share my inner self completely. This has been a source of some sadness.

As I had written off the world of boys and men, I embraced the world of girls. I generally found their approach to life much more appealing and managed to cultivate some very close friendships at school. One in particular was called Sue, although her friends called her Billy. She was an ex-girlfriend from my carefree, pre-Pink-Perm days, who I didn't treat very well, but luckily she had a very forgiving nature. Through her I became friends with her friends (another Sue, who they called Henry, and Kate) and became almost the only boy regularly welcomed into the girls' common room in the sixth form.

Ironically this also seemed to bring me some status amongst my male peer group. I thought they would bitch that I had found my true place amongst the girls as I was girlish myself. Instead they marvelled at the fact that I could just go up to girls at the school disco and start talking to them. The rest of my friendship group huddled against the wall and were too tongue-tied to ask a girl to dance. So their reaction was more jealousy and grudging admiration. In fact they became convinced that I was a raging Casanova having sex with every girl in town. This was far from the truth. I always had a girlfriend, it was true, usually a very pretty one, but I was a very slow developer sexually and was still a virgin when I left for college. Still my refusal to confirm or deny their speculations meant that the myth only grew.

By the time my school days ended I had regained a lot of my earlier confidence and it certainly seemed as if my strategies for life were working. OK I had a strained relationship with other men, but my ease with women compensated for that and gave me the kind of friendships I felt I needed and lots of nice girls to date. My academic achievements were getting me where I wanted to go – to London to study engineering. Surely years of good mental health awaited me.

In fact during the three years at university I also flourished. I overdid the studying a bit in year one, but eased off a bit after that and achieved a better balance. I had a good group of male friends on my course who I kept at arms-length emotionally but who provided a good social life. I had close female friends including my best friend and first love, Anne. I was happy and thought I was in good shape.

The problems emerged when I started work. Compared to the constant intellectual stimulation of university, work seemed to comprise doing the same thing over and over and I was soon bored. Without the regular affirmation of my intelligence by passing exams I became a slave to my perfectionism and stressed over getting everything absolutely right. My determination not to show any males (and in engineering they are mainly males) a sign of weakness meant I was hiding my uncertainty and not asking for help. Fear of failure was ensuring that I didn't fail, and indeed started to succeed again, but it was taking its toll.

Many people will experience anxiety in their first jobs, so I was not alone in that respect. However I am convinced that the emotional intensity of my fear of showing any sign of weakness linked back to feelings I experienced while being bullied. I was determined never to be picked on again, but the strain of being on alert for any signs of attack was draining.

The tell-tale signs of anxiety and depression set in at about 26. I was working on the best job I ever had – the Channel Tunnel – with an amazing team of high-flyers overseeing the design of the tunnels. I was the youngest in the team but was keeping up with them and amazing my immediate boss and mentor with the mature way I was dealing with difficult situations. What he didn't know was that at some points in the day I scurried into the toilets shaking with anxiety and taking deep breaths to try and calm myself and get back to my desk.

We worked long hours, then often retired to the pub after work. I oscillated between the thrill of being part of such an operation and massive attacks of imposter syndrome. I had constant gastric problems and could feel my stomach clench as negative thoughts forced themselves to the front on my mind. I learned to push them back down, almost swallowing them, so I could get on with what I was doing. In time I could do this so quickly and effectively that I began to feel almost nothing at all. The Iceman had cometh.

Anne coined that phrase as she saw her Squidge (the embarrassing pet name she used for me at the time) disappear to be replaced by an unemotional robot who seemed incapable of loving her the way he used to. At first he only stayed for a few days before the Squidge returned. Eventually however he took up semi-permanent residence and then even I began to question whether I loved her the way I used to do. Sadly it led to us breaking up for several months. The pain I felt when she moved out removed any doubts about my love and luckily

I persuaded her to give me another chance. For ten more years I struggled on, seeing doctors about my constant stomach trouble, having tests which yielded nothing and a supposedly final diagnosis of Irritable Bowel Syndrome (IBS) caused by stress. I was told to take it easier and improve my diet. Not once in that time did anyone mention mental illness.

I would like to deviate a little from my main point here to reflect on that IBS diagnosis. At the time I was disgusted with this outcome and could not believe that all the problems I was having could be caused by what sounded like a trivial complaint. I was really suffering and was sure I had ulcers or cancer or some other serious affliction. I was almost disappointed that I was not seriously ill as this would have given me a valid excuse for taking time off work to recover or to argue for a lesser workload. Instead I was just a man who couldn't handle stress as well as other men and who had an upset tummy like a little child with bad nerves. Of course I would not have been any happier if the root cause had been identified as mental – I still had a long way to go in my education of such things.

Today, like most people, I have a much better appreciation of how important gut health is to our general wellbeing and how debilitating IBS and other intestinal problems can be if left untreated. Such conditions can make normal life almost impossible. We are also much better informed about how our mental and physical health are linked and affect one another. If you have received a similar diagnosis please do not be as foolish as I was. Do not dismiss it as trivial and try to overcome the stigma which still remains around both bowel movements and anything which is linked to mental illness.

I did manage a few breakthroughs on my own. I realised that the perfectionism, which was possibly a success factor in exams, was pointless and harmful in the work environment. However hard you work on something as a junior, when your boss receives it he (it was usually a he) takes out the red pen as he proves his virility and justifies his position by making changes. I embarked on a project I called "doing things badly". Instead of aiming for my usual 100% I forced myself to do an 80-90% job and hand that in. To no-one's surprise but my own, the work was to a perfectly acceptable standard and I got brownie points for delivering more quickly. It took me a while to get used to this.

The funniest example was when I was entered for a competition that I didn't really want to do. I had to submit an extract of a paper, then if I got through that stage to prepare a draft paper, and if I was shortlisted to write a paper and present it at the Institution of Civil Engineers. I tried to do a bad job at every stage, in the hope of getting kicked out, but failed miserably. My inability to present poor work meant I won the competition. There was still room for some personal growth there but I was taking a bit of the pressure off.

I also realised that my refusal to show any sign of weakness was making me intimidating to others. I caught a young female engineer doing unpaid overtime on one of my projects because she was terrified of being late or overrunning the deadline. She saw me as a hard man who would not tolerate weakness in others. From that day I tried to present a more human face in work (to incorporate some of the softness and kindness I showed in my private life) and became not only a better manager but a more popular colleague.

Despite these small improvements my health declined and by my late thirties I was struggling so much with life, trying to follow this advice to reduce my exposure to stress, that I considered giving up my role as a Director and becoming a delivery van driver. Something was clearly seriously wrong. It took my wife to point me in the right direction.

Voice 1:	"I am looking forward to the next bit."
Voice 2:	"Why – is it finally the end of this drivel?"
Voice 1:	"No, it's the bit where I get to talk about Anne."
Voice 2:	"I don't know why she puts up with you."
Voice 1:	"I guess because she loves me."
Voice 2:	"Another mystery. You don't deserve her."
Voice 1:	"I know I am very lucky to have her."
Voice 2:	"Lucky she doesn't leave you. Then you would fall to pieces."
Voice 1:	"No. I am stronger than that – thanks to her."
Voice 2:	"Oh please – this bit's going to be really soppy isn't it?"
Voice 1:	"Yep. You will just have to suck it up."

5

Behind Every Happy Depressive….

If you were to ask me to name the single biggest contribution to me remaining a happy depressive, I would not hesitate to answer. Her name is Anne and she has been holding my hand every step of the way.

The summer sun was high over Purley Hill – an oasis of green amongst the urban sprawl around Croydon. Housing developments were creeping up the hill on all sides but left enough greenery around the footpath to fool strollers that they were in the countryside. The birds sang, the hedgerows sprouted a few berries, and all was calm.

Anne had dragged me off the couch and out of the house to try to shake me out of my habitual Sunday mood. At the time I was travelling once a month to the Far East, either Singapore or Taiwan, to oversee projects for Mott MacDonald, and I was continually jet-lagged. At the weekend I just wanted to collapse and recover, and on Sundays I brooded over the fact that Monday loomed and I had yet to regain my energy.

"Isn't this nice?" she said. "Getting out the house and enjoying a bit of fresh air."

"Yes, love. Thanks for the kick up the arse."

"Maybe we should make this a regular thing?"

"Sure, if the weather cooperates."

"People can still walk in the rain you know?"

"I suppose."

"Or we could take a long weekend. Go walking in the Peaks maybe, you used to love that."

"We could, but to be honest I am sick of travelling. I just want to rest."

Anne stopped walking. I turned and saw her start to say something, then change her mind. We walked on in silence.

"Let's sit here for a while," she said, pointing to a bench. "There is something I need to tell you."

She sat and patted the space beside her. Slowly I joined her, then turned so we were both looking out at the view.

"I don't think I can carry on like this pet." She swallowed hard and started again.

" I love you to bits but I am beginning to resent you. Well not you exactly but the fact that Motts are getting the best of you and all I am left with is a burnt-out shell of a husband."

I kept staring straight ahead, afraid to look her in the eye.

"You're clearly not enjoying the job but you are pushing yourself to the limit. Why for God's sake?"

"Because it's my job. That's what I do."

"You don't even get pleasure out of things you used to enjoy. When was the last time you did any drawing? Or wrote a story?"

"I don't get the time."

"Of course you do. You lie around all weekend like a zombie. I do my best to help but I am at my wits' end. I think you need professional help."

"I tried that, remember? I went to that MIND group thing, but they were all in terrible shape. I'm not that bad."

"So is this how you want to live the rest of your life? Because I am sorry but it's not how I want to live mine."

The penny finally dropped. I was not only risking my health, but I was also risking the most important thing in my life. We had been together 20 years and if I wanted another 20 or more years with this wonderful woman I had to change something. I had to admit I was ill.

Two weeks later I sat with my GP, a new guy who I hadn't had much to do with until then. I described my physical symptoms and my hectic lifestyle and told him I was "a bit run down". I still couldn't say the words, but he could.

"How are you feeling mentally?"

"What do you mean?"

"How is your mood?"

"Not great. I am very tired."

"Any negative thoughts?"

"A few."

"Thoughts of self-harm?"

"No, no, no. Nothing like that. Just a bit low that's all."

"How long have you been feeling like this?"

"About six months I guess."

"Do you think you are depressed?"

" My wife certainly thinks I am - which is why I am here."

"Well, I think she may be right. So I want you to see our psychiatrist."

"OK."

From there things progressed quickly. The following week the psychiatrist gave me a questionnaire to see where I fell on the spectrums of anxiety and depression. I was high on both. He asked me to think back to when such feelings had first begun. They dated back to my late twenties, on the Channel Tunnel project. He prescribed the first of many anti-depressants, which I swore I would only take for a few months. Soon after, I met Harry, the lovely guy with the amusing hairpiece who would teach me the techniques of Cognitive Behavioural Therapy (CBT). I was officially mentally ill – but I was also on the road to recovery. Without Anne I am not sure I would ever have taken that step.

We met when I was 18 and she was 19 (for six months of the year I am her toy boy). It was an inauspicious beginning. I got off with one of her girlfriends who was down from Yorkshire to visit her in London. Anne was busy one night so her two friends attended a fancy-dress party (come as a song) at my student house (two doors down from Anne's). Despite being dressed as "The Lumberjack Song" from Monty Python, in a checked shirt, heavily stuffed bra and a pink pencil skirt, her friend Monica seemed to fancy me. The next day I went around to Anne's house in the hope of linking up with Monica again. While I was allowed to accompany them to Oxford Street it soon became clear Monica didn't fancy me without the skirt, but Anne and I were hitting it off pretty well. At Monica's suggestion they gave me the slip in Top Shop so I went home alone, but it was no longer Monica on my mind.

Luckily we had a friend in common (the one who had lent me the pencil skirt) so our paths soon crossed and the connection between us became obvious. On the 11th January 1980, at the Life Sciences disco in the junior common room, I managed to grab Anne for a dance (she had arrived very late after going to a Blondie concert).

On the dance floor I said, "Can I ask you a personal question?"

Apparently she was terrified that I was going to say, "You fancy me don't you?" and then tell her we should just be friends. But she said yes anyway.

"Would you like to be my girlfriend?"

Again the answer was yes, and two became one.

Anne and I are rare examples of the thing we are told to strive for in our romantic lives – soulmates. I don't actually believe that for every person in the world there is that special person who completes them - "the One" that many people search for. More accurately there may well be such a person, but the chances of meeting them are vanishingly small. For the very lucky few it happens, but if that is set as the benchmark for happiness most people will end up disappointed.

Yet I do believe that the core of what Anne offers for me is a necessary part of being a happy depressive: a safe space where I can be entirely myself without judgement. This doesn't have to be with a soulmate or even with a romantic partner. Research has shown that a close group of platonic friends can be even better for one's mental health than a romantic relationship. If you do not have access to such a group there are many online communities now related to mental health. They are a great place to vent those pent-up feelings safely, and other people going through similar difficulties will be there to offer comfort and support. They can also help to spread the load even if you do have that one special friend to call on, so that you don't overload them or become too dependent on them.

Depression and anxiety can often lead us to cut ourselves off, to shut out the wider world in the hope of reducing the stimulae to a bearable level, or simply to avoid having to put on our "game face". (When I am depressed, for example, I find it very hard to answer a ringing telephone). When we do venture out the strain of appearing "normal" in our interactions with others can be enormous and leave us drained at the end of a bad day. Of course getting home to spend time alone also allows us to drop the façade and to relax somewhat. If that is all that is available then spending time on self-care can maybe be enough, but don't embrace that self-sufficiency too readily. A partner, friend or family member who knows the full you, warts and all, and will still be there with a hug and unconditional love is a massive boost to your chances of being happy. This is a precious resource and if you are lucky enough to have it do not push them away, even when you can barely talk and just want to hide under the duvet.

Equally important is to nurture that resource by not taking it for granted or abusing it. If you have a life partner or friend who is always there they will see you at your lowest points, when the influx of negative thoughts temporarily overwhelms you. At such times the temptation to lash out at the world becomes very strong, and those nearest to you can end up in the firing line. It will happen occasionally so forgive yourself for that but make sure you apologise as soon as you are calm again. Give them time to forgive you if they are hurt and tell them how important they are to you. Also look out for the signs, which you should be expert at spotting, that they are feeling low and not in the best place to help. Treat this as time to repay the debt and care for them when they need it too.

Just as you will need time to learn about your own condition and how to cope with the negative thoughts or a run of bad days, so will they. Be patient and try to help them understand how to help you (maybe buy them a book like this one). A big lesson for them to learn, both to help you but also to sustain your relationship, is that your low mood is nothing to do with them. In fact it may bear no relation at all to what is going on in your life. If they love you they will try to solve the problem, to look for reasons for your sadness and to suggest ways to end your pain. It can be very hard for them to accept that sometimes there is nothing that they can do except sit with you while you ride out the storm. It took Anne many years before she believed that my emotional withdrawal (what she nicknamed The Iceman) was not caused by a problem in our relationship or a reduction in my feelings for her but my difficulty in dealing with feelings at all, which I coped with by shutting down. Thanks partly to her help The Iceman has been banished for good but it took me a while to get there.

The Happy Depressive has to do a lot of self-work to protect themselves from the effects of depression, but if you don't have to do it alone then the chances of success are, I believe, that much greater. I hope you too can find your safe space where you can be yourself without judgement and where love and support are available to you.

Voice 1:	"Time to deal with the pills next."
Voice 2:	"Well you should know all about them you addict."
Voice 1:	"Anti-Ds are not addictive."
Voice 2:	"So why can't you stop taking them?"
Voice 1:	"Because I need them."
Voice 2:	"Because you can't cope with life without them."
Voice 1:	"I could, but it would be so much harder. So why stop?"
Voice 2:	"You are just weak. Or lazy."
Voice 1:	"Nice try but I am not buying that."
Voice 2:	"So what is your excuse?"
Voice 1:	"I don't need one. The pills work for me and allow me to achieve what I want to achieve."
Voice 2:	"Which is what exactly – being too doped up to feel anything?"
Voice 1:	"Nope. To live a normal life. To be a Happy Depressive."

6

The Pills
(warning: it gets a bit sciencey)

If you suffer from depression you will probably have to develop a relationship with the pills prescribed to you and, like many relationships, it can be complicated.

When I was first told I needed to take anti-depressants I was very resistant to the idea and was adamant that I did not want to be on them for the rest of my life. When I told my mother her reaction was:

"Oh no, you don't want to be on them for the rest of your life."

She was right, I didn't, but why did we both jump to that reaction? I often draw parallels between depression and diabetes, which I will come back to, but had I told her I had type 1 diabetes, and therefore would have to inject insulin for the rest of my life, her reaction would have been different. She would still have been sad for me but would never have suggested that I should stop taking the insulin. The aim with anti-depressants however was clearly to get off them as soon as possible.

The main reason, sadly, is the stigma attached to mental illness. If you have diabetes society will consider you unlucky, worthy of sympathy, and worthy of respect for carrying on with life despite this handicap. If you have depression then you are judged by the same people as somehow culpable for bringing it on yourself, by not dealing with life very well. They believe that once you have managed to "pull yourself together" it will go away again.

We who suffer tend to absorb this message even if it is not expressed bluntly to our faces. It was many years before I could face the common question "and are you taking any medication?" without hesitating to tell whoever it was (even if it was a massage therapist I would never see again) that I took anti-Ds. I hesitated because I felt ashamed.

This shame around depression, like many other things society makes us feel about ourselves, is misplaced. Going back to my diabetes analogy, that is an illness clearly caused by a physical malfunction – the inability to naturally produce enough insulin. Insulin is a hormone which allows us to use sugar to produce energy. Diabetics have to inject themselves with insulin because their pancreas does not make enough naturally for their body to function normally.

Serotonin also acts as a hormone and is a neurotransmitter which carries messages between neurons in the brain. When serotonin levels drop, some of these messages are not transmitted correctly, and low serotonin levels are believed to affect both mood and sleep. It would not work to inject serotonin into the brain, so the class of drugs I am most familiar with act by reducing the rate at which serotonin is reabsorbed into the neurons (i.e. they inhibit the re-uptake of serotonin and increase the levels in your brain) while leaving the rest of the chemistry as untouched as possible (i.e. they are selective). For this reason they are known by the snappy name of "selective serotonin re-uptake inhibitors" or SSRIs for short.

I learned this bit of brain chemistry while taking my first course of pills and I am afraid I did not immediately conclude "well that's alright then, I will keep taking these as long as I need them". The internalised shame was still strong, and so I tried several times to stop taking them, even though that always proved to be a mistake.

At the time I was first diagnosed, in 1997, two older classes of anti-depressants, tricyclic and monoamine oxidase inhibitors (MAOIs) had fallen out of favour due to their side effects and risks of overdose. It is unlikely that they would be prescribed today except in special cases. SSRIs were all the rage, the most famous being fluoxetine (sold as Prozac) which had been around for about a decade. I was prescribed Seroxat (paroxetine) at a dose of 20mg per day.

For the first two weeks the side effects were unpleasant (nausea, frequent headache, dry mouth and a strange involuntary clenching of the jaw) but not that hard to bear. Soon the effect on mood kicked in, including some periods of euphoria where I could not stop giggling. They were quite fun but it is probably a good job they wore off as the Project Director giggling uncontrollably in meetings would not have gone down well. After two months everything had settled down and I would say my mood was consistent, with no major lows but also no major highs. I have read about some people who felt so emotionally flat on Seroxat that they stopped taking it as they felt like a zombie. I was relatively content however that the really painful feelings had gone and I was in a better place to learn my cognitive behavioural skills.

After about six months I convinced myself that I was cured and asked to come off the pills. My GP advised against it so we compromised on another 3 months so that the withdrawal period would be over a holiday break. This first time the withdrawal was not very bad, rather like the acclimatisation period in reverse, and initially I was confident that I wouldn't need them again. Unfortunately over the next 6 months my anxiety and depression gradually returned to levels similar to those before my diagnosis. It was a slow decline with a succession of highs and lows but each time the lows got a little deeper. While the CBT allowed me to divert the negative thoughts quite effectively, it did not stop them from coming and the effort of dealing with them was gradually leaving me more and more drained. I went back to the GP who proposed the obvious solution.

In the year or so that had then passed Seroxat had also fallen out of favour. It had been shown to cause suicidal thoughts in young people and other serious side effects in a minority of cases (Prozac suffered similar bad press). Though I had experienced no such difficulties the doctor was no longer recommending Seroxat so I was prescribed sertraline (sold as Zoloft or Lustral) again at 20mg.

After a similar acclimatisation period (this time with milder symptoms) things settled back to a situation similar to that on Seroxat, though I thought I had a slightly wider emotional range. In this stabilised state I entered psychotherapy in an effort to find the origins of the negative feelings and to see if I could cut them off at source.

I got some pressure to come off the pills from the therapist, which surprised me, but I resisted. Some therapists seem to believe that you cannot fully connect with your feelings while you are medicated. This must be a theory developed by someone who has never experienced depression. If they had they would know that for those like me the mental turmoil is way too distracting to engage properly with therapy. For the next two years sertraline kept me thinking clearly enough to do the self-analysis needed to benefit from that therapy.

At that point, just before my 40th birthday, I decided on a major career change and my wife and I moved to Luxembourg where I would work for the European Investment Bank (EIB). I faced a new job, in a bilingual environment when I didn't speak the required French, in a new country, and leaving my friends and family behind. Despite this overload of change I was feeling confident that I had now cracked the depression problem so I discontinued both the pills and the therapy. Yes I appreciate that does sound a bit reckless.

The withdrawal from sertraline was considerably worse, either because of the drug or because I had been on it longer. Long after the drug had left my system I experienced "the zaps". This is a feeling mentioned on all depression forums but not acknowledged by doctors for some reason. It is so-called as it feels like someone is administering a small electric shock to your brain, and it almost but not quite has a noise to go with it (you feel a kind of jolt near to your ears). At its worst this can happen several times a minute and completely ruins your concentration.

Doctors will tell you that after two weeks there is no drug left in your system so it can't be causing this symptom, but my fellow sufferers and I are convinced that this is caused by the body trying to adjust to the lack of its serotonin fix. With me it lasted about three months and it was very hard work to carry on normal activity. When the withdrawal was finally over, and it was time to assess how the mood was doing, I was already slightly weakened. That, plus the huge stresses of the changes I was facing (I became so terrified of sitting in meetings in French and not knowing what was going on that I came the closest I ever got to a panic attack) meant that I was in a bad way pretty quickly. So it was back to the GP.

This time it was an English woman of advanced years who seemed disdainful of anti-depressants (and depression in general) but acceded to my request and gave me escitalopram (Cipralex) instead of sertraline, for reasons I never determined. I would be on them for the next eight years. Luckily I soon moved to a different doctor, who was a joy to work with. He and I varied the dose of escitalopram between 20mg and 40mg depending on how I was feeling over those years. Not once did he make me feel bad about needing a higher dose and I was beginning to shed my shame about having depression. This proved to be a good thing as it was about to go a bit more public.

A situation had developed at work which brought daily conflict. A more senior colleague had decided he wanted to remove me from my post, but as I was doing very well in that role he went down the "constructive dismissal" route of making my life so unbearable that I would leave. I was determined not to give in but of course over time my physical and mental health suffered. I reached my lowest point ever and in the end my GP signed me off work for six weeks to recover.

The GP wanted to try me on a different drug in case the escitalopram had become ineffective (and a particular side effect was beginning to bug me) so I switched to this new one. I am afraid I can't remember the name as I was in a bad way and these pills made me worse. I became incredibly angry and short tempered. One day I was sitting in my car and something happened to frustrate me – I can no longer remember what the trigger was. I lost control and smashed my fist down on the central console of my car (a lovely Jaguar coupe). I broke the leather armrest and the cubby hole beneath it which never worked properly again and was a daily reminder of those times till I sold the car.

After two weeks I stopped taking that one and moved onto anti-D number five – citalopram (sometimes called Cipramil but my pills are just called, refreshingly, Citalopram). That was sixteen years ago. I did try going without the pills one more time, after I retired, to see if the removal of work stress would mean I could cope without them, but again without success. Now I accept I will be on them, or some form of anti-D, for the rest of my life.

When I returned to work I told HR that the cause of the escalation of my illness was this colleague and that I wanted to move jobs, which I did a few months later. I also told all my team that I was off with depression. By then I was forty-seven and I was sick of hiding it. If you go into work struggling with a virus you don't hide that fact from colleagues, and maybe even feel a little pride at soldiering on through your illness. If you are having a bad day mentally, with potentially a bigger effect on your abilities, why do we hide that fact and feel shame?

I have learned to be grateful for the help the pills give me in living a normal and happy life, but the main reason that the GP was switching pills and that I tried once more to come off them was one really annoying side effect. It is a side effect that was listed in the directions that came with all five of the SSRIs I took, but which is rarely discussed publicly because it touches on another taboo – sexual dysfunction. For this reason I would like to explain this side effect in some detail.

SSRIs have a potential side effect on sexual function because the increase in serotonin, which clearly has lots of benefits, unfortunately can also desensitise the sex organs. Most of the warnings in the literature usually refer to loss of libido. I have never suffered that, or at least any effect has not been noticeable. I can only imagine how that would affect someone who is already depressed. Very depressed people do not tend to feel very sexy, but if the pills are working to improve mood and as a result the opportunity to start a new relationship opens up, it must be very difficult to then find the sexual drive is not there.

For me the effect of SSRIs is different and is much more rarely discussed in the literature. My libido seems fine, and I have no problems achieving or maintaining an erection, but the pills interfere with my ability to ejaculate and reach a normal orgasm. This is, I believe, due to that desensitising effect (and I found a few academic papers which suggest the same). All five SSRIs had the same effect but it gradually got stronger over the years. No doubt this was partly due to age but it could also be an effect of prolonged use of the drugs.

Initially the effect was just to delay my orgasm, which up to a point was actually a benefit. The first casualty was blowjobs. After a few years I could no longer reach orgasm that way, which was a disappointment to both my wife and I, but I could do so through penetrative sex so it was not the end of the world. Next my ability to come during sex became intermittent, with lack of orgasm occurring more frequently over time until, by my late fifties (so about twenty years on the pills) I never reached full orgasm through sex. When I stop taking the pills the problem goes away and I climax every time, so there seems little doubt that it is the pills, combined with the effect of aging, causing the problem.

Both my wife and I agreed that in order to keep the depression at bay it was a price worth paying, and we learned to appreciate sex in a different, less goal-oriented way. I can understand why, for some people, this and other side effects make taking the pills unbearable and they try to manage their depression in other ways. I wish these people the best of luck, but for me I accept that I will always need them and no longer feel any shame in taking them. Don't let shame push you into stopping the pills if they work for you as they do for me. Life is sweet when the chemical balance in your brain is under control. And if we have to we can live without blowjobs.

And more pills

When I started writing this book I had planned to end the chapter on pills here, but life had other plans.

I had been struggling with my depression for about eighteen months. I did follow my own advice and go to the GP to adjust the dose a few times, so had gone up to 40mg at one point. I was also starting to suffer from very bad insomnia, but it was inconsistent. I could have a run of up to seven days where I could not get off to sleep, often finding myself up at 3 or 4 in the morning, knocking back a whisky in an attempt to calm my restless body. I would get so exhausted that I could barely function, my sporting activity became too much of an effort, and I was having several really bad days in a row. Looking back I feel foolish for not questioning whether the citalopram had ceased to be effective, but there was a complicating factor.

At the start of this bad period I lost my father. There is probably no nice way to lose a parent, but I think the way Dad went was one of the cruellest. He was diagnosed with both Alzheimer's and vascular dementia and suffered a long slow decline over five years. Towards the end he still recognised close family but couldn't remember what he or they had said minutes before. Talking to him became an endless loop of mundane questions and answers and it became impossible to reach the man he used to be. Once the diseases took his emotional control and started to limit his physical abilities it was very painful to watch. In the end of a bout of pneumonia saw him hospitalised. To rub salt in the wound COVID restrictions meant that he was in hospital for weeks without us being able to visit, and by the time we got in to see him he was so diminished, scared and confused that our hearts broke and we felt the end was nigh. He died a few weeks later.

Though I felt some relief that his suffering was over I was clearly grieving and found it hard to separate my genuine sadness from the effects of depression. Voice 1 and Voice 2 were both down in the dumps, so I was very slow to attribute my feelings to the depression and I knew it was best not to try to medicate away my grief.

About six months into this period I went to a sleep therapist and had a battery of tests, including an overnight test monitoring my sleep patterns once I was off. Despite the fact that I was very restless when I tried to go to sleep, I did not have the usual marker in my blood tests (low ferritin) which indicated a condition known as "restless legs syndrome". I had mild sleep apnoea (an interruption of normal breathing) especially when lying on my back. This could explain why I was so tired, as apnoea can reduce the depth and quality of sleep, but nothing could explain why it took me so long to fall asleep in the first place. I kept a sleep diary but one week I could follow the rules of sleep hygiene rigorously and still have a bad night, then the next week break all those rules and sleep like a baby. It made no sense and had no pattern. A bit like my depression - so maybe I missed a clue there.

I struggled on for another year but when writing this book and while doing some research to back it up I started to feel that I knew what the problem was. There were a number of articles and papers suggesting that citalopram was known to stop working, sometimes quite suddenly, if taken for a long time (classed as more than a year). That could be happening in my case. Restless legs syndrome was also a potential side effect of SSRI's. Though I had not suffered from that greatly in the early years I had always been a restless sleeper (as Anne can testify). Was it possible that long term use was also making this worse?

I started to look into alternative drugs and reading papers on their efficacy and side effects. I thought that while I was at it I would also study their recorded effects on sexual dysfunction as that had been the most annoying side effect for the past few years. My research found two candidates that seemed promising – vortioxetine and mirtazapine.

Vortioxetine came to my attention mainly because it showed some promise on the sexual dysfunction problem. I read a meta-analysis (a paper that summarises and compiles lots of other studies) of the effects of different anti-Ds on sexual dysfunction. Vortioxetine showed lower effects on both erectile dysfunction and anorgasmia (not coming) compared to SSRIs. It was a comparatively small study – too small to draw firm conclusions – but it looked hopeful.

Mirtazapine had the potential to solve both my sleep problem and the sexual dysfunction. It causes drowsiness in most of the people who take it, so it is advisable to take it at night. It works in a different way to SSRIs as it doesn't work on the re-uptake of serotonin but acts to make the communication in the brain more effective. So maybe the desensitising effect would be diminished.

Armed with this research I contacted my GP. Like many people who use the NHS I belong to a group practice where you do have a nominated doctor but unless you are willing to wait months you normally get to see whoever is free first. In this instance I asked for a call back from my nominated doctor, who is a wonderful and patient person, and I got lucky. She was free within a week.

Now, a sure-fire way of annoying most GPs is to turn up armed with all the facts you got by Googling your condition and telling them what you think your diagnosis is. If you do this – and I think you should have the right to do so if they are not coming up with any ideas themselves – prepare yourself for a bit of kick-back, but be assertive. Also avoid being aggressive. Most GPs are great people who are only in this tough job because they care, and even the poor ones have probably been worn down by a failing system.

I refreshed the doctor on my conditions. (In this computer age I always have the fond hope that when I see a medical practitioner my full medical history will be up on a screen in front of them, and that they will have scanned it before talking to me. Somehow I still always have to tell them my medical history again.) In brief these were: "I can't sleep; I can't come; and I am depressed." I then gently explained what I had found online and asked what she thought. She was very sweet and didn't get annoyed with my Google Doctoring. In fact she asked if I had a medical background so I must have sounded convincingly knowledgeable.

She explained that vortioxetine was not normally prescribed in general practice. In the UK at least it was usually reserved for psychiatrists to treat major depressive disorder. She didn't rule it out but thought my other suggestion was more promising.

Mirtazapine was available through general practice and in her view was good for people who had trouble sleeping. She also thought that my restlessness at bedtime could indeed be caused by the citalopram. She was less informed on its effect on sexual dysfunction but agreed that as it was not an SSRI it had a chance of helping there too. She warned me that it is notorious for increasing appetite and that many people taking it gained weight. I decided that was a minor concern. If it worked I would be sleeping well, feeling happier and could keep my weight down by having lots of sex.

Another advantage of mirtazapine is that because it does not increase serotonin directly it allows cross-tapering. This means you do not have to fully come off the SSRI, and suffer the full effects of withdrawal, before taking the new drug. It also works more quickly than most SSRIs so the benefits of the new drug should kick in sooner. We agreed I would drop the citalopram from the 30mg I was taking to 20mg for the following three days, then down to 10 mg for four days, then stop altogether. I could start with mirtazapine at 15mg (the lowest dose) straight way, taken just before bedtime. So that is what I did.

On day one I took my 20mg of citalopram in the morning and mirtazapine about 10pm, anticipating a bedtime of about 11pm. By about 10.30 I had really strong restless legs and couldn't even lie still on the sofa, which was pretty disappointing. By 11pm this had worn off so we went to bed, with me feeling quite drowsy (and a little wobbly on my legs) and I went straight to sleep. That was more like it.

The next day I definitely felt over-medicated and fuzzy, and continued to feel like that for the first week. I started to take the evening pill earlier, to make sure the legs calmed down before I wanted to sleep, and I continued to get off very quickly. After a few days the intensity of the urge to wriggle also dropped off. I tried to play tennis as usual, but the over-medicated feeling made it hard and though I made it through an hour I was much more tired than normal.

Even at 10mg of citalopram the over-medicated feeling persisted but once I had gone down to zero that feeling stopped. The second day on zero SSRI was my first amazing day for several years. That day I wrote the piece "Today" at the front of the book and felt superhuman all day. I was rushing around trying to find extra things to do with this newfound energy and motivation and I loved every minute of that day. I was making the most of it in case it didn't last. It didn't.

The day after that the zaps started, and they continued up until the day I was due to speak to my GP again, two weeks after we started the switch. Strangely though, I didn't get that upset about it. I didn't feel great but Voice 2 was pretty quiet and Voice 1 was telling me this was just a temporary problem. So the mirtazapine was not only helping me sleep, it was maybe also being effective against the depression. Two out of three problems addressed then. What about the other one? Well I am delighted to report that my wife and I tested the effect of my new pill on sexual dysfunction and it had completely disappeared. It was as if we had turned the clock back twenty-five years.

When I spoke to the GP again it was of course not my doctor but another one I had never met. I explained everything again, reported that the signs were that all three problems might well be solved with the new drug, but I was having trouble with the zaps. To her credit she did not dismiss these out of hand. She admitted she had never heard of them but was Googling as we spoke and she got thousands of hits, so she believed me when I told her that this was a well-known phenomenon in all but the medical field. (In fact since I first started trying to convince doctors of their existence a few medical studies on causes and severity of the zaps had been done).

She said she would read up on them when we finished the call. So I risked another suggestion. I told her that the last time I came off citalopram, on a really long taper over several months, the zaps only appeared after going from 5mg to zero. Would she have any objection to me trying 5mg in the morning combined with 15mg mirtazapine? She didn't, as long as I was sure this wouldn't bring back the sexual side effects. I was pretty sure it wouldn't (and again I am delighted to tell you I was right).

I tried this regime for several weeks. (I was delighted to see on the citalopram packet the instruction "to be taken daily to prevent the zaps".) The zaps did abate but there was still a feeling of slight disorientation along with a feeling that a zap was about to come. It was only really noticeable when I tried to play tennis. I was struggling to move in time to connect properly with the ball. This was annoying but did not outweigh the other benefits.

I had one or two nights when I couldn't get to sleep at my normal time, or awoke early, so ended up with five or six hours sleep. Unlike before, this sleep seemed to have been better quality, as I didn't feel exhausted the next day. I had become a regular afternoon napper in retirement but that urge seemed to have gone.

At the next check in (with yet another doctor) I told them about the continued problem with the disorientation. I was convinced this was still a withdrawal effect – partially suppressed zaps. It could also have been a side effect of the new medication mirtazapine. The doctor advised coming off the citalopram completely but on a very long taper so that we only had one drug to consider and diagnosis would be simpler. I considered this but decided that making the doctor's life simpler was not my top priority. So I increased the citalopram back to 10mg. The feeling of disorientation disappeared. So 10mg citalopram in the morning, 15 mg of mirtazapine in the evening is the new (hopefully final) regime.

I am now back where I like to be – stabilised on a correct dose of anti-D where I can cope with the residual effect of depression using the strategies I describe later on. This time I am not troubled by insomnia or sexual dysfunction so life is even sweeter. So far I have only had two truly amazing days, but many others have been good to great. I am occasionally so happy that I feel the prick of tears in my eyes and spend much of my time in a state of contentment that has been missing for years. It sometimes feels too good to be true, and maybe it will prove to be. So I will enjoy every minute of it. I have recalibrated, in the short term, my expectations for the ratio of amazing, good, poor and really bad days. I have also prepared myself for the scenario that this turns out to be a honeymoon period between me and mirtazapine, so that I will not be crushed if that proves to be the case.

But I needed to modify my closing line for this chapter. We can indeed live without blowjobs (or your own preferred form of oral sex) – but it is really nice when we don't have to.

Voice 1: "I should cover the fact that not everyone takes pills."

Voice 2: "Yeah, not everyone is a junkie like you."

Voice 1: "I mean that they do not work for everyone."

Voice 2: "Makes your book a bit of a waste of time then, eh?"

Voice 1: "No, there is plenty of other good stuff in here."

Voice 2: "Like what?"

Voice 1: "The important thing is to calm one's mind enough to apply the coping strategies. And to keep you quiet."

Voice 2: .....

7

Or Not the Pills

In the previous chapter I spent a lot of time extolling the virtues of anti-depressant pills and the important part they have played in my life. This is because they have always worked for me – but what if they don't work for you? Sadly they do not work for everybody. For SSRIs the reported success rate depends on which papers you read but very roughly it seems that they are effective (meaning they reduce depressive symptoms by about 50%) in around 70% of people, and lead to complete remission in 30-40% of cases. Clearly that leaves about 30% of people for whom the effect is between zero and 50% of their symptoms being relieved.

There is also the issue of the side effects, which are responsible for many people discontinuing treatment. When I get a new medication I tend to scan the list of possible side effects very quickly but pay it little attention. The manufacturers will list every conceivable side effect to protect themselves from litigation but in my view run the risk of putting many people off taking the pills altogether, as some of the side effects sound truly horrendous. Luckily they are also very rare. I view the list as handy to have if you develop a new symptom to see if it might the be the pills causing it. In my case only the very mildest of side effects bothered me in the first two weeks of taking them, with only the sexual dysfunction effect being long term.

For the unlucky few, however, the side effects can be very serious. Some SSRIs have increased thoughts of suicide, particularly in younger users, and need to be discontinued pretty sharply. For some people they reduce depression but increase anxiety; make them so sleepy they cannot function; cause weight gain which can complicate other physical or mental issues; or seriously upset the stomach. For younger people setting out on new relationships the sexual dysfunction may be a deal breaker. For others, particularly those who need the maximum dose, along with the lows the pills have removed the highs and the emotional flatness leaves them feeling like a zombie. They do not feel like themselves and stop taking the pills to regain a feeling of being in control again.

If you face one of these situations and have discounted taking pills as part of your solution then that is fair enough. The main message from the previous chapter was that you should not stop taking the pills, particularly when they are working, out of misplaced feelings of shame over your condition. Think like a diabetic – it is a pain having to take them, but I need them. If they are not working then there is little point in taking them. At the same time I would urge you not to give up on treatment too soon. There are quite a few different types of drug which have proven to be effective, and though you probably were offered SSRIs as the first port of call, it may be that one of the others suits you better. It now seems that even for me SSRIs were not the best bet and mirtazapine was waiting there for me all those years.

You may have what is termed treatment resistant depression, an unusually self-explanatory medical term. If you have failed to respond to between two and four drugs prescribed through general practice you may be referred to a specialist. They can try less common drugs, alone or in combination, to give you that little bit of chemical support to make all the other coping techniques easier. I appreciate it can be hard to keep the faith with the medical profession and it requires a lot of patience and resilience when things are not working. You may have decided that the path of taking drugs to control your condition is just not for you.

Does that mean that there is nothing in this book to help you? I hope not. I know that I could survive if the pills did not work for me either. It would mean that the negative thoughts would come thicker and faster, that Voice 2 was stronger and that I would need to ramp up the energy put into my cognitive behavioural therapy (CBT) and self-analysis in order to control them.

I would probably look into various techniques for calming the mind in order to somewhat replicate the effect the pills have in giving me those extra few milliseconds of thinking time. Though I have not needed them personally I have friends and family who have had success at using such techniques. Breathing techniques such as castle breathing are very calming and particularly good for anxiety. Yoga can help both mind and body together. Various grounding techniques (using focus on your environment to bring a sense of calm) and mindfulness can be effective for many people. One relative of mine uses the Three Principles or 3Ps technique to stop the negative thoughts from inducing panic and to remain calm, and finds keeping a journal really helpful.

If these techniques proved to help less than the pills I would need to adjust my targets for what I think I could achieve in a day. During my working years that would have had an impact on my productivity, maybe even my career progression, but I believe I would still have managed a good life balance and overall happiness through my other strategies. I hope that you can achieve the same.

Voice 1:	"Time to tell them about Harry."
Voice 1:	"What is it with you and that guy? You should call this book 'When Harry met Steve'."
Voice 1:	"He taught me something I use every day."
Voice 2:	"So?"
Voice 1:	"And he was very kind."
Voice 2:	"You're pathetic."
Voice 1:	"Shut up. I just needed someone like him at that time for me to believe CBT would work."
Voice 2:	"So are you gonna put on a silly wig as well?"
Voice 1:	"No I will just tell people how it works for me, and hope it works for them too."

8

CBT

I first met Harry about two weeks after I had seen the psychiatrist. He was one of those people whose resting face was a half-smile. His deep brown eyes spoke to me of kindness. I would guess he was in his thirties, as I was then, with a youthful face and full, smooth cheeks. It would seem he had gone bald at a very young age as he wore a wig. It was one of the worst wigs I had ever seen. The quality of the hair was probably fine, but there was way too much of it, especially on top. It looked more like the hair of an Elvis impersonator than a young Indian man.

I cannot think about Harry without smiling to myself. Not just because of his wig, though it did amuse me for a while. The wig just added to his humanity. It indicated his own insecurities to which I could relate, being very proud of my own hair. He exuded warmth and empathy and offered a lot of reassurance to someone who was highly sceptical of what we were about to do. For Harry was about to introduce me to Cognitive Behavioural Therapy or CBT.

At that time, the late 1990s, CBT was the only treatment offered on the NHS. Demand was relatively low so the waiting time was very short. Today the NHS offers more choice of talking therapies but you will find it still favours shorter forms which are seen as more cost effective than open-ended therapy. The waiting times have gone up but are reported to be four weeks in most cases for CBT, and this is still likely to be the first thing offered (as well as online courses).

Harry started off by asking about my negative thoughts and how they made me feel. By this time I had been suffering from depression without a diagnosis for about ten years. My survival mechanism had been to recognise when the thoughts came and to repress them. Something would trigger my negative response, I would feel that clench in the stomach and tightness in my chest, then I would use my strength of mind to push the thoughts out of the way and get on with whatever I was doing, usually my job.

Harry acknowledged the strength of mind this technique required, and said that was a positive thing which would help me master CBT. Repressing thoughts in this way may get you through the day, but he said there is usually a price to pay in physical symptoms. This I could confirm as my IBS was very bad at this point.

For the next few weeks he wanted me to try a different process. When a negative thought arose he wanted me to live with it long enough to examine that thought and see what feelings it generated in me. Initially I was to write them down when I could. He gave me a printed form to complete with four columns. The first two columns were for the negative thought itself and the feelings it generated. The third column was for a reframing of the negative thought in a more positive way – for example an alternative interpretation of events that had generated the clench to the stomach. Column one was the domain of Voice 2, column three was a chance for Voice 1 to have his say. I was to write down one or more alternatives to the negative thought and then in the fourth column write down how I was feeling about that version of the thought.

At the time I remember thinking, "Is that it?" To me it seemed too simplistic to be effective, but I had really taken to Harry and wanted to please him, so I toddled off with my form full of good intentions.

For the first few weeks I did OK at filling in the first two columns but the third was proving tricky. Harry assured me this was normal. After all for the past ten years I had believed these thoughts were real and were so terrible that I had to supress them. I had let Voice 2 get the upper hand. Harry helped me by offering potential alternatives himself and if one of them struck me as valid I wrote it down.

Let me give you an example. At the time I was a Principal Engineer leading projects and reporting directly to the Project Director. On one project that director was Tony, who was newly promoted. I had known him for over ten years. He had been the lead engineer on the designs for the Channel Tunnel that I was managing for the contractor. At that time I was his client and we had a very good working relationship. Now I was working for him and it was not going well. He was micro-managing and checking everything I did, sometimes giving instructions directly to my team. Voice 2 was telling me that he didn't trust me, maybe even that I had somehow offended him years ago and this was payback time. This was making me angry, anxious and frustrated.

Harry had an alternative explanation to put in column three.

"You say he is newly promoted?"

"Yes."

"And you used to be his client?"

"Yes."

"Back then did you feel he thought you were good at your job?"

"It certainly seemed like it."

"So try to put yourself in his shoes. He has only just been made a director. He knows the job you are doing inside out, because that was his job until very recently. However he is very unsure of what to do in his current job, so he is slipping into his old role which is more comfortable. He may also see you as a highly competent manager who could do his job better than him and is feeling insecure so wants to assert himself as the boss."

It took me a while for this to sink in but it made just as much sense as my interpretation so it went into column three. Harry hadn't finished.

"Does that interpretation reflect badly on you in any way?"

"Er, no."

"So how do you feel now?"

"Well if it is true, I feel much better of course. His problem is not with me, it is with himself. But how do I know which interpretation is true?"

"You don't, but why focus on the most negative one?"

Why indeed? In fact in this case that was not enough for me so I invited Tony for a coffee. I said I was a bit concerned about how closely he was supervising me and asked if he had any concerns about my abilities. Then it all came pouring out of him. He fell over himself to reassure me that he knew I was perfectly capable but was struggling to adjust to his new role. It was exactly as Harry had surmised.

I was so glad I asked. Not only did it massively improve my confidence in CBT but it massively improved my working relationship with Tony and we became a bit of a team. He would ask my advice on aspects he was unsure of and I would do the same. We both benefited from a healthier working environment.

Spurred on by this success I diligently filled in my sheet for the next few weeks. The pills were also starting to kick in so the rate at which negative thoughts arrived was reduced and examining them became less painful. I was getting the hang of this and couldn't believe how such a simple technique could be so effective. The sheets were a bit clunky though.

About four sessions in Harry told me I probably no longer needed to write everything down, just to practice the technique in my head. He was right I could do it, and much more quickly, and I noticed the clench was much reduced. I was not as afraid of the dark thoughts as I had been before.

I think we had six sessions in all before Harry thought I no longer needed him. I still think of him, and thank him for the technique I use every day. I can now do it so quickly in my head that on good days it is almost subconscious.

It is only fair to mention that at that time I had a good friend who also suffered with depression and who had also been through CBT training. She was not surprised that it worked for me – as she put it a "hyper-rational engineer". She could see that the logical approach would appeal to me, but it didn't work for her. She could not manage the step of overriding the strong feelings by a logical reframing of the thoughts. Her Voice 2 was too strong (and she wasn't finding the pills as effective as I was). In fact she has tried so many different forms of therapy over the years, none of which has worked, that it would seem her condition is very resistant to such methods.

If CBT doesn't work for you there are other techniques offered. A modification of CBT called Acceptance and Commitment Therapy or ACT is now offered on the NHS in the UK. Rather than challenging the negative thoughts this concentrates on accepting your thoughts and associated feelings without judgement. It has elements of mindfulness to focus on the present moment. The aim is to help you move forward through difficult emotions to allow you to put your energy into healing instead of dwelling on the negative. I can't recommend this from personal experience but have met people who found this very helpful.

In my first few months of using CBT I got so proficient that along with the beneficial effects of the pills I convinced myself that I was cured. So I stopped taking the pills.

Life was to prove that CBT alone would not do the trick.

Voice 1:	"Its psychotherapy next."
Voice 2:	"That sounds like fun."
Voice 1:	"No, not fun, but useful."
Voice 2:	"But it's just paying someone to listen. Don't you have any friends? "
Voice 1:	"Yes, plenty."
Voice 2:	"So why can't you bore them with your problems."
Voice 1:	"Because they will just give me advice."
Voice 2:	"Isn't that what you want?"
Voice 1:	"No, I want someone to listen, without judgement, and help me to find my own solutions."
Voice 2:	"That'll never work."
Voice 1:	"Ah, but it does. It works just fine."

9

Psychotherapy

After being on the antidepressants (Seroxat this time) for about nine months, and feeling confident in my mastery of CBT, I felt better than I had for many years. I felt like I had cracked this depression thing and stopped taking the pills. The withdrawal period was short and not too painful and for a while I thought I was going to be OK. Then the slow spiral back into depression began.

The thing about CBT is that whilst it may help you deal with the negative thoughts in a healthier way, it doesn't necessarily stop them coming. And dealing with them, even once you master the technique of doing it quickly in your head, takes energy. With the help of the antidepressants the rate at which the negative thoughts arise is slowed down, even on the worst days. On the best days I hardly need to deal with them at all. However, once I stopped taking the pills, Voice 2 was gaining in strength and Voice 1, even with CBT in its corner, was struggling to keep up.

As the months passed I was getting progressively more tired. My sleep was affected, my concentration was poor as I was increasingly involved in using CBT for crisis prevention, my IBS came back with a vengeance and I was soon taking time off work with repeated viral infections (which were my body's way of crying out for a rest). After about nine months I went back to the doctor and restarted the pills (sertraline this time).

Once I had stabilised a bit I started to consider psychotherapy. My logic was that I needed to discover why the negative thoughts were occurring, and why they had such force, to try and cut them off at source. Again I had to overcome a major internalised prejudice against therapy. I thought of people who went to therapy as weak, as people who could not cope with life without a crutch. Similar to my earlier views of antidepressants. I am glad I overcame this prejudice. Mental health is at least as important as physical health and I would not hesitate to seek help for a physical illness. I now see that refusing help for a mental illness is a form of self-harm.

I discovered that the company I worked for had a scheme by which employees could access short term psychotherapy at zero cost – limited to six sessions. Everything was confidential. So I applied.

My allocated therapist was a guy up in central London so I travelled up from Croydon to see him once a week for six weeks. Initially I was a bit disappointed by him. After Harry I was expecting warmth and a feeling of affection, but I found him a bit cold and reserved. We sat quite far apart in our chairs and there was a definite formality about proceedings. He was small and dark and very difficult to read.

I understand that a short period of counselling can be useful for some people and for some problems, but it does put limitations upon what can be achieved in the time available. We spent two weeks exploring what seemed to be my problems and identifying priorities. Then we focussed on those priorities for a few weeks before needing to wrap up. We both agreed I was going to need longer term therapy.

No more free help was available so I started to look for a private therapist. I found a woman quite near where I lived and booked a series of weekly visits with no pre-agreed end date. She was in her fifties and had the air of a school headmistress. Again I had to overcome my disappointment. I think I had assumed therapists were all touchy-feely types who might give you a big hug at any moment. Maybe Harry had spoiled me for the rest of the profession. Therapists from the psychodynamic school, as I was using, feel it helps to maintain a certain emotional distance which, in retrospect, I think is right.

As I laid out in the first chapter we got a bit diverted for a while searching for repressed memories in my poorly remembered early childhood. Once we got off that we made good progress.

For several sessions we talked about my early life in the periods that I could remember so that she got a good understanding of my background and the emotional landscape in which I grew up. Obviously we talked about the bullying episode at school which was a significant development in my emerging personality but we also touched upon other areas, which I had not previously thought of as significant.

For example I recalled being very distressed by my parents arguing. Looking back they were the normal arguments which occur even in the happiest of marriages but at the time they scared me. Like many children I wondered whether I was somehow the cause of this conflict and assigned myself the role of peacemaker, trying to come between them to stop the fight. I had forgotten this feeling but it turned out my subconscious mind had not and certain circumstances in adult life could cause very similar emotional stress.

The sessions began to follow a particular pattern. She would ask me to relate experiences in my recent past which had triggered negative feelings and ask me why I had reacted in a certain way. She would then challenge me by suggesting an alternative reason for my reaction, often making reference to childhood experiences which might have affected my response. I would respond by rejecting her alternative interpretation (which to me sounded like an accusation of behaving in a childish manner) getting a bit annoyed and then being told to go away and think about it. By the following week's session I had come to realise that she was probably right, admitted so and then we could move on. In a similar way to CBT we were building up Voice 1, giving it a few more muscles to fight off Voice 2.

We did this for nearly two years and I learned a huge amount about myself in that time. Whenever my reaction to a certain situation, usually at work where I seemed to be the most sensitive, seemed out of proportion I would imagine the conversation with the therapist.

"Was that reaction proportionate to what happened?"

"No."

"Why do you think you reacted that way?"

"I don't know, I just got really angry."

"Don't you think it has similarities to [insert childhood experience here]?"

Answer then, "No." Answer one week later "Yes, I see what you mean."

I then found it easier to react to situations in a way appropriate to the older, healthier, more confident me. Like CBT it got easier and quicker over time.

My psychotherapy ended when I decided to move to Luxembourg at the end of 2000. Or at least my formal sessions with a counsellor ended. My informal sessions with my internal counsellor, Voice 1, continued and I got better and better at conducting these sessions at the speed of thought.

Now I was equipped with an armoury of three weapons: the pills plus my internal therapist, who worked in tandem to slow down the negative thoughts and spot the times when old trauma was being triggered, and the CBT to neutralise the thoughts that got through the primary defences. It didn't always work and it always took a lot of energy but I now felt I had the tools to cope and that true happiness was within my grasp.

Voice 1:	"Time to put this all this together into a plan."
Voice 2:	"Are you still persevering with this book idea?"
Voice 1:	"Yep. I am on to coping strategies now."
Voice 2:	"And why should anyone listen to you?"
Voice 1:	"Because I have been doing this for decades and I have learned a lot."
Voice 2:	"That don't make you no expert fella."
Voice 1:	"I don't pretend to be. I am trying to be that friend who shares their experience in the hope of helping others."
Voice 2:	"As they say – with friends like you, who needs enemies."
Voice 1:	"I think we both know who the enemy is here."

10

How To Cope – While Working

I was probably forty-one by the time I had all the tools needed to fully combat my depression. I had accepted I would probably always need the pills and my CBT skills were finely tuned. After two good years of psychotherapy I understood my condition and how I responded to certain situations, plus I felt confident at self-analysis. I hope that if you are in the same boat as me you will reach this level of preparedness much earlier in life. Maybe this book will help.

Of course I did not have to wait forty-one years to be happy. There were lots of high points in my life up to that age. My wedding day is still the happiest day of my life, I had my overseas adventures in the Far East and Middle East through my work, I had a great romance, good relations with my family and some good friends. In between the moments of joy, however, was a lot of struggle from day to day, and what I wanted most, but could not achieve, was a sense of peace and contentment with what was objectively a very nice life. It was like taking a hike through the most breath-taking of landscapes carrying a 50kg backpack. You can still appreciate the beauty of your surroundings but you long to put your burden down and take a rest.

From my late twenties I was tired all the time, had constant problems with my digestive system, frequent bouts of apparent viral illness, headaches, dizziness and nausea. I sought physical diagnoses for all these problems and when they failed to appear, apart from the consolation-prize diagnosis of IBS, I thought of myself as weak and incapable of dealing with the stresses inherent in the kind of career I wanted to pursue.

It got to the point where I believed that being a delivery van driver was more appealing than continuing in my role as a director of a major consulting firm. (What a disaster that would have been as I need so much intellectual stimulation to stop myself getting bored that I would have gone mad in the first week.) Thankfully I sought help before making such a stupid career move. Instead, while in a good stable condition, I realised that I did not enjoy the director role (and all the internal politics that went with it) as much as I had my previous role as project manager. So I moved to work as a technical adviser in a bank in Luxembourg. This turned out to be the best move I ever made.

As I said before I foolishly tried to start this new phase of my life pill-free, which was not a success. Once restabilised on SSRI number three I developed a way of coping that served me well until I retired seventeen years later. In that time I again became a manager of teams (up to 25 people at peak) this time engaged in providing expert technical advice both to the Board of the Bank and to the governments and administrations of the new Member states who joined the EU after 2004. It was still a relatively high-pressure job, with its fair share of workplace politics to endure, but it suited me better and generally I coped with it very well.

Before I explain my approach it is important to explain one caveat. I made a decision that I was never going to take sick leave due to depression alone. Maybe it could be argued that I still had not fully accepted my illness and continued to harbour some shame about it. There is probably some truth in that, as I still wanted to keep my depression private. I genuinely believe that if you need to take time off to protect your mental health that is what you should do (and in one extreme instance I did). I also believe that if you want to maintain a career in a senior position, as I did, then you cannot necessarily rely on your employer taking this enlightened view. I loved my new job and I was fairly sure that if I took time off every time I felt depressed I would not be given the responsibility I wanted. Part of me also did not want my condition to define my life so strongly. So I took a different approach, which may not suit you. Your depression could be more severe, for example, or you may put much less weight on professional success than I did. If, like me, you want to cope with depression while still holding down a difficult job, then this approach may be for you.

When I am working the first thing I do upon waking is try to decide what type of day it is going to be. In the background the CBT and self-analysis are always working away to divert and reassess negative thoughts, but the amount of effort they expend and the proportion of my energy they use up depends on the type of day.

The rarest of days, for me, are those where I awake fully refreshed and bursting with energy. These days are precious, and maybe it is a shame to waste them by going to work (I should probably compose an opera or run a marathon) but if I do go to work then I get a lot done and all my interactions of the day are infused with this energy. Let's call those my amazing days. Sadly, I might get one or two of those a month if I am lucky. I doubt anybody gets these every day.

Much more common are good days where, once I have shaken off the sleep and moved fully from the last dream into the reality of the day, I realise I feel OK. No negative thoughts come rushing in and I don't feel shattered. I can get out of bed promptly and get myself off to work without having to push myself. I feel calm and composed and can work well. The key thing on such days is not to overdo it. The sign of the right dosage of pills is when such good days form the slight majority of my life rather than becoming rare (at which point action is needed – usually a slight increase in pill dosage). A long run of such good days can make me complacent, however, and I run the risk of taking on too much and working too hard leading to a downturn in my health. Pacing yourself even when you feel pretty good is important for maintaining good mental health.

In my experience almost as common as the good days are what I term poor days. On such days, once fully awake, my all-systems check identifies that things are not great. I am very tired and getting out of bed seems like a big hurdle. I feel low, unmotivated, mentally sluggish and can't face the thought of dealing with people. I start to think of all the things I have to do that day and it seems overwhelming.

The first thing I do on a poor day is avoid rushing out of bed. It is important not to panic. I give myself an extra ten minutes or so to try and compose myself, think about the day ahead and see how important the day's task list really is. This might make me a bit late for work but I will arrive in better shape for it. I find that poor days can go one of two ways.

Sometimes, once I am up, dressed and into work, I find that as soon as I have to interact with other people and start to conduct the business of the day the depressed feeling goes away. Or at least I become so distracted by work that I don't feel the pain. Such days can turn out to be pretty productive, almost on a par with a good day. I would say these account for about two thirds of poor days. They are pretty tiring, which suggests to me that the background work depression requires is taking its toll, and I usually collapse on the sofa in the evening pretty worn out. Nevertheless I feel good about making it through the day.

The other third of the poor days don't go so well, and going to work doesn't snap me out of the depressed or anxious state. These days are a bit more of a grind and I do my best to protect myself. I try to avoid difficult interactions if I can (though this is not always possible) as I am more prone to over-reacting in this state. I try to clear some of the easier and more pleasurable tasks on my list (even if they are not the most urgent) and have some playtime interacting with my favourite people (even if the excuse to see them is a little flimsy). Basically I accept that anything I achieve that day is a bonus, and I can make up for lost time on the next good day. This was the hardest bit of my approach for me to learn and adapt to. It is very easy for other people to trigger my conscientious side by pushing me to address things they believe are urgent (for them). In time I learned that most things can be deferred a little until I am in better shape without the world coming crashing down.

Then there are the bad days. On such days as I emerge from the dreamscape into the real world I experience a kind of dread. I get the clench in my stomach even before I have had time to form coherent thoughts. My weariness is off the charts and even conversing properly with my wife is a strain. These are the days when answering a ringing telephone fills me with an irrational fear. I do not want to face the day.

If they fall on a weekend or holiday, as they sometimes do, I tend to spend at least the morning in bed attempting what I call a "reboot". Quite often, when I wake up feeling this terrible, going back to bed after breakfast, lying down and spending a few hours trying to calm my mind can reboot my brain. I might or might not fall asleep but I manage to soothe the pain and when I get up again later I can be in pretty good shape. The technique is a form of meditation I guess. I avoid thinking about my depression, often distracting myself by replaying in my head some rubbish we have watched on TV the night before, or by engaging in a pleasant fantasy. When it works I have salvaged half a good day. Sometimes, sadly, it doesn't work and the day is a write off. This is when I say I have to stop fighting and let myself go down to the bottom to bounce up again.

These are also the days when many would argue that I should take a sick day – and I wouldn't completely disagree. So what happens if it falls on a workday? Well in my case, because of the decision I made, I still get up. It may take a long time – I will certainly be later than

10 minutes that day – but eventually I find the strength to run through the morning routine and head off to work. Then I struggle through the day, leaving as soon as I can and doing as little as possible, telling myself that they are lucky I am there at all. I console myself (using a good strong Voice 1) that I am so productive and good at my job on other days that one lost day will not make a real difference. I also console myself with the knowledge that these days are rare. Tomorrow is probably going to be better. Usually it is.

I would say that when the pills dosage is right and I am stabilised the bad days are one or two a month. They often follow a period where I just could not avoid overwork due to particular work pressures. In my case it was often when overseas work missions got crowded together and I had too many flights, nights in hotels and poor night's sleep in a row. On occasion it was because I had partied too hard but then at least I had the pleasure before the pain. Sometimes it is just the random nature of chronic depression and a bad day comes out of the blue. If these days get to be more common than once or twice a month then it is time to go back to the doctor, adjust the dosage, or maybe try a new pill if the old one has stopped working.

So that was my strategy for those seventeen years. I took a different approach to the day depending on whether the early morning check predicted an amazing, good, poor or bad day ahead. Most of the time I was able to adjust the work to match the mental capability I had on a given day. Obviously in any job there are lots of external pressures which don't always cooperate with your plans, and when that happened I had to (or chose to) grit my teeth and worked through it. Sometimes I got enough rest in the evenings and at the weekend to recover from this extra effort. Sometimes my body would rebel and I would have a few days off with a physical illness, usually a virus, before returning to work. But most of the time it worked and I completed the successful career I loved.

You would be forgiven for being disappointed with this approach. You may be thinking "is that as good as it gets?" or "it doesn't sound that great", but we have to face the fact that depression is going to have an impact on our lives. What it doesn't have to do is define what we can achieve. On amazing days we can enjoy our superpowers. On good days we can enjoy our full normal powers. On poor days we give ourselves a break and don't push ourselves too hard unless we are forced to (and then we take our rest). On those few really bad days we either hide under the duvet seeking a reboot or struggle through knowing that days like this are rare. Most of the time we are on the upside of the deal, so we should not waste the good days worrying about the downside. As I say, it worked for me, except for one time. It is only fair that I also cover the period when external factors meant that this strategy couldn't work, as this may happen to you too.

Around eight years after joining the Bank I was doing the job I loved most, running a large team of experts working in 12 different countries who were advising the new member states. I had built this team up from nothing and was doing a great job. Unfortunately in doing so I had made a dangerous enemy. He was several grades more senior than me in the organisation and was politically much better connected than I was. He was not my direct boss but had the power to make my life very difficult. In my opinion he was hopelessly inadequate at the job he had been assigned. Foolishly I did not try very hard to hide this opinion and I am therefore partly to blame for the fact that he took such a dislike to me he wanted me out of the way. He started a campaign to get me removed. He never admitted it to my face, despite me challenging him several times, but over a period of about three months I kept finding out he was briefing people against me and proposing organisational changes which would undermine my position. Eventually it became clear that he was likely to get his way, and I was effectively going to be demoted without ever getting to argue my case to the decision makers. At that point the strain became too much and every day was proving to be a bad day for weeks on end. I went to see my GP, explained the situation, and got signed off work for six weeks with depression.

It was not a problem of dosage or failure of any of my tools or my coping mechanism in this case. I was facing a situation which most healthy people would have found intolerable and which was dangerous for a person with depression to try and tolerate. So I took a break and put my mental health first. In some ways I found it a relief that my diagnosis was out in the open and I suddenly felt I could admit it to friends and colleagues without shame. When I did so their reaction was overwhelmingly supportive. I sought a transfer away from this toxic situation, which I got a few months later and for the remaining nine years at the Bank the above strategies proved adequate again.

The principles of how to cope cover both cases:

- Get to understand the severity of your condition.
- Learn to spot the patterns to know when things are amazing, good, poor or bad.
- Set sensible limits on what you try to do that day based on your capabilities.
- Do your best to listen to Voice 1 not Voice 2.
- When external pressures make the situation overwhelming for your normal coping strategies put your mental health first and take a break

These principles got me to the age of fifty-seven at which point I decided I could afford to retire and that I had done enough in my chosen career to feel satisfied. I imagined that, as most of the triggers for my depression seemed to revolve around work, in retirement my depression would abate somewhat. I even hoped that maybe it would disappear entirely. This just proved that as yet I had still not fully understood my condition, and that a new coping strategy was just around the corner.

Voice 1:	"Time to deal with the challenges of retirement."
Voice 2:	"What's so hard about lounging around and playing golf?"
Voice 1:	"In theory nothing. In practice it's a big adjustment."
Voice 2:	"Good God man, you are never happy."
Voice 1:	"I am happy, but I needed to find a new way of being me."
Voice 2:	"Who wants to be you? Have you thought of being someone else?"
Voice 1:	"No thanks, I like being me. I just had to rediscover what that meant."
Voice 2:	"Please tell me you are not going to bang on about finding yourself."
Voice 1:	"You will have to read it and see."
Voice 2:	"No thanks – I am going to watch some paint drying"
Voice 1:	"Please yourself."

11

How To Cope – With Retirement

I think most of us who work will dream, at times, about our retirement. Whether the job is boring, physically taxing or stressful there are days when the idea of stopping work and putting our feet up seems like heaven. For those of us with depression it holds out the hope that maybe, without the daily stress of work, life will get much easier.

There are also people who identify so strongly with their work persona that the idea of retirement is anathema to them. They often tell you they love their jobs, and for a lucky few that may be true, but I have also encountered people who just seem to have got the work balance very wrong. They have developed so few interests outside of work that they have become what they do not who they are.

I fell somewhere between the two. I remember telling my dad while I was still at college that I would be a director at thirty and would retire at fifty having made a million pounds. I am not sure where I got these ambitions but I suppose they were some nice round numbers to aim for. I gave little thought to what I was going to do from the age of thirty to fifty. Would I remain a director for all those years? Would that allow me to earn my million? I certainly didn't think what I would do in my retirement or wonder whether one million was enough to last if you retired that young. Luckily by the time I did retire I had a more mature approach, but I still did not have all the answers.

Though I did love my job and had enjoyed my career I knew it took its toll on me and a rest seemed very appealing. I was also being subjected to another unwelcome reorganisation so it seemed a good time to leave. I had interests outside my job that I wanted to pursue but I was also worried that I would miss the stimulation that work provided. I started to plan, months before I left, voluntary activities which would keep me occupied for two to three days a week but still leave time for my leisure activities. Surely this was the time to get the golf handicap down to single figures at last.

I felt like I had a good plan in place and left work pretty confident I was going to thrive in retirement. It was certainly better than having no plan at all but the adjustment was harder than I had anticipated.

The first pleasant surprise was that I didn't miss my job. After the initial shock of suddenly having no emails to deal with, and no meetings to attend, which felt very strange, I hardly thought about work at all. At least not while I was awake. For some reason in my dreams I was often still working and the dreaming version of me often thought "why am I doing this – I am sure I was due to retire last month". I am still trying to work out what that means.

What I did miss was the clear self-image I had developed for myself through work. I was the maverick manager who really looked after his team, and earned their loyalty and trust. I was also the one to challenge the senior management when they did things, usually for reasons of internal politics, which negatively affected my team or the work they did, and the one to defend them against external criticism. As a result I was very popular with all those who worked for me and with me, and slightly unpopular with many in senior management. This interfered with several promotion opportunities but I didn't really care. To me my integrity was, by then, much more important than career progression.

I also had a clear social identity outside of work. Anne and I were the great party hosts who would hold the annual Stroll and Sausage. This was an event where we would organise a beautiful walk through the forests or vineyards of Luxembourg, followed by a massive barbecue party at our house. At its peak we had almost a hundred friends attending, which still wasn't all the people we invited.

Then, when I left the Bank and Luxembourg, that all stopped. I was back in the UK with my friends, colleagues and clients all in other countries. Worst of all I was no longer entirely sure of the answer to the question "Who is Steve?".

There was a bit of a delay to the emergence of this existential crisis purely because we were busy. For the first year Anne and I had to find a temporary home to rent while we sold our house in Luxembourg, then look for and purchase a property in the UK. We had cars to sell, new ones to buy, removals to organise and spent lots more time with our parents now we were "home". I was also deploying my plan. I trained to be a pastoral support worker with the UK Humanist organisation (so that Chaplaincy teams in prisons, hospitals and universities could offer non-religious support) and as a celebrant who could officiate at naming ceremonies and weddings. I enjoyed the training and felt for a while that life was really on track. So much so that I once again tried to come off the anti-depressants.

You would have thought by now I would have learnt my lesson. I was no longer motivated by shame as I had got used to being open about my depression, so why did I stop taking the pills? There was some logic to the decision. I was feeling good, could take rest whenever I needed it, was doing more sport and getting fitter and I thought the conditions were the best they had been for a long time. I was irritated by the sexual side effects which were worse than ever. Plus I just wanted to see whether work stress had been the primary initiator of the physical and mental changes leading to my depression. It seemed worth a try.

I spoke to the GP and we very slowly reduced the dose of Citalopram over 3 months. I felt pretty good all the way down to 5mg per day, but as soon as I went to zero the zaps started and stayed with me for several months. Once fully clear of withdrawal it was time to see how I was doing mentally. That is when the issues around retirement really began to show themselves.

One big area of change when one or both partners retire is that they get to spend a lot more time together. Anne and I were pretty confident that this was not going to be a problem. We love each other's company and had bemoaned the time apart that my job had required, so we expected this to be a big bonus. Instead we found ourselves arguing a lot about trivial things – especially housework.

While I was working and out all day and away some nights Anne had taken on the brunt of the housework so that we could spend all our free time at weekends on fun activities. She only worked on occasional temporary jobs so this seemed the best division of labour. Clearly once neither of us was working we would have to divide this work more evenly. We were both surprised at how many arguments this seemed to generate. After a few months we went to see a counsellor specialising in couples therapy to help us sort this out.

We only went once but it helped us to understand that in a way I was now an interloper in an environment that had been Anne's domain for a long time. She had her way of doing things and would get stressed if I was doing them differently. She also wanted me to take more initiative and do things without being asked, but I was so out of practice I didn't always realise things needed to be done. In the end we solved the problem quickly enough, but it highlighted that change, even one you expect to go smoothly and be a positive, can cause strife you are not expecting.

A much more serious problem was me struggling to find my new identity. This manifested itself mainly in me starting and then stopping various voluntary activities because they were not giving me the satisfaction I sought. In part this was because I was approaching them in my old work persona as someone who set very high standards and was used to challenging areas of inefficiency and ineffectiveness.

I didn't pursue the pastoral care role because I didn't agree with the way it was implemented in practice, I spent weeks training to be an advisor with the Citizens Advice Bureau and then gave it up for very similar reasons, and started working with two organisations doing workshops in schools. With the last two the main problem was that their activities were based too much in London and its surrounding areas rather than where I lived, but I would still fume about the organisational failings I perceived them to have.

I was really struggling to accept that the voluntary sector is going to be different to the sectors in which I had previously worked, and to mould Work Steve into Volunteer Steve. Volunteer Steve needed a different set of skills and I found it hard to let go of the skills I was most proud of, and which propped up my self-esteem in my working life, to develop a softer skill set appropriate to my new role.

I had my answer to my question. No it was not just the stress of work that led ultimately to my depression. It was the challenges of life, and retirement was throwing up just as many of those as work had done. The depression wasn't going to disappear, the pills would still be needed and coping strategies would still need to be devised.

If you find yourself struggling in retirement it is important to let yourself off some hooks. The specific stress of work may have gone, but other factors out of your control can still trigger your depression and continuing to seek the support of medication and therapy when necessary is simply good self-care.

As we age most of us will encounter other health issues which can add to the difficulty of life. Not long after resuming the anti-Ds in retirement, and just as I was starting to feel better, I was diagnosed with a very rare auto-immune disease affecting my eyes (and threatening my sight). I had to endure six months of systemic immune-suppressant drugs which made me sick as a dog before the specialists found a better treatment that was effective. At times like these we will all need our tools and strategies. The good news is that retirement does make those strategies easier to implement.

Going back to our grading of days into amazing, good, poor and bad, we have much more scope for accommodating the latter in retirement. Whilst I chose to drag myself into work on the bad days, there is no point in struggling like that anymore. I had quite a few bad days in the first few years, either during the withdrawal or during treatment for the eye problem, so the number of duvet days and attempted reboots was significant.

It is not nice having bad days but I have really come to appreciate the freedom that retirement offers to just roll with them and wait for them to pass. I have become pretty good at distracting myself for the whole day if necessary with mindless pursuits (reading and social media are great for that) and taking the opportunity to rest. It would be going too far to say that I enjoy a bad day, but I enjoy the fact that I can give myself the gift of that down time. Very few things in retirement are so urgent that you need to push yourself to do them on such days.

On poor days the substitute for getting up and going to work, in order to distract myself and force me to "fake it till you make it", is sport. There has been many a poor day where I have sport, usually tennis or golf, scheduled and after the morning all-systems check I am less than keen. Because I know that it works most of the time I usually get up, get in the car and drive to the club. The combination of interacting with people and expending energy almost always helps me to shake off the low mood. If I don't have sport scheduled I will go for a drive in my sportscar or a ride on my motorbike. If none of these work I revert to the strategy for a bad day and hope for better the next morning.

On the good days I would still recommend pacing yourself a little, but it is much less of an issue because if you overdo it you can have a lovely rest the following day.

My retirement is now divided into two periods: BM and AM. BM stands for before mirtazapine. For the first five years I was on citalopram. I now realise that along with dealing with the change overload retirement can bring, the joys of a global pandemic and a bereavement, I was also dealing with a drug that was becoming less effective. I struggled on, probably longer than needed, with the ratio of good to bad days being very poor. My strategies helped me cope but I now think I should have sought help sooner.

In the AM era however it looks as if the pattern is going to be much different, with both bad and poor days being much rarer. On good and amazing days I now have so much energy, particularly mental energy, that I am having to learn how to cope with this new version of Me. I am having to regulate my behaviour more, as I can get a bit exuberant and sometimes fall short of the standards of cool I set for myself. I also find myself hunting around for the next thing to do to use up this extra energy. My strategies for this new phase are still developing but it is a nice problem to have, and while my medication is in the sweet spot I plan to make the most of it.

It may not last but if those gloomy days become more common again, I know how to cope.

Voice 2:	"Why are you depressed anyway?"
Voice 1:	"What do you mean why?"
Voice 2:	"Well look at you. Your life is cushy."
Voice 1:	"True, it is. I am not complaining about my life"
Voice 2:	"Yes you are. This whole book is one long complaint about being sad."
Voice 1:	"You are definitely missing the point."
Voice 2:	"Which is?"
Voice 1:	"Depression can strike anyone – even the lucky ones."

12

Not Guilty

One of the bits of ad-hoc advice friends and family often give to depressed people is to look on the bright side and "count your blessings". It is probably well intended and it is not in itself bad advice. I do often remind myself of all the ways in which I am lucky in my life and sometimes this helps me to accept the downsides more readily. But it is also the proverbial double-edged sword. If you are really depressed despite acknowledging all your advantages this can make you feel worse.

Research has shown that a number of life factors will increase your chances of suffering from depression. The Centre for Mental Health, part of the Commission for Equality, has published statistics on a number of determinants which can have a negative influence on mental health. Men and women from African-Caribbean communities in the UK have much higher rates of post-traumatic stress disorder and suicide risk than the general population. People who identify as LGBT+ have higher rates of most common mental health conditions and lower scores for wellbeing than heterosexual people, a gap which is greater for older adults and those under thirty-five. Children from the poorest 20% of households are four times as likely to have serious mental health difficulties than those from the wealthiest 20%. Women are ten times as likely to have experienced extensive physical and mental abuse during their lives, and those who have had such experiences show high rates of attempted suicide, self-harm and homelessness.

I have none of those disadvantages. As a white man I suffer none of the negative consequences associated with ethnicity. Ironically, given that I was called a queer at school when I was not questioning my own sexuality, it turns out that technically I qualify as queer. As my sexuality developed over time I came to realise I was pansexual, but as I can easily pass for a straight man this has never caused me any problems in adult life. I grew up in very modest circumstances in a working-class home on a council estate, but I never experienced real poverty. Though I have suffered some of the effects of toxic masculinity this pales in comparison to the damage it does to many women.

Running through a checklist of my privileges is healthy in one sense, as it improves my empathy towards those who are less fortunate. When I am very depressed and down on myself, however, it can encourage Voice 2 to tell me that I am an ungrateful wretch with no good reason for being depressed. Being depressed despite all these advantages can feel like a character flaw – and some ill-informed people might view me that way.

At such times it is important to realise that wealth and privilege do not protect you from mental health problems. One only needs to scan the media to see thousands of cases of the rich and famous who struggle with their mental health. Depression does not need a reason to strike you down, and it is through no fault of your own that it picked on you.

You are not guilty. Let yourself off that particular hook, seek the help and support you need and believe that you are just as deserving of that help as the next person.

Voice 1: "Okay, as you think all I do is complain here are the upsides."

Voice 2: "Now you want them to believe being miserable is a good thing?."

Voice 1: "No, but dealing with depression does have its benefits."

Voice 2: "Best of luck selling that one."

Voice 1: "I think that is the nicest thing you have ever said to me."

13

The Upsides

If I were to bump into our local genie tomorrow, and he was handing out wishes, would I ask him to banish my depression for ever? Yes, I would. It is true that I am currently in a love affair with mirtazapine and the effect depression is having on my life is the lowest it has been for many years. Even so, there is an effect and the prospect of the new pills becoming less effective is always there. Though I know I will cope if that time comes, it would be great not to have to make the effort.

If the genie had the power to make it so that I had never had depression, and offered me that wish, I think the answer would be no. Yes it would have been great not to have had the struggle over the past thirty-seven years. I am bound to wonder what else I might have achieved with all that extra energy. At the same time there have been positive developments which are a direct result of my depression, and I would not want to wish them away.

The first and most obvious one is that it led me to seek therapy. Of course, I could have gone to therapy without having depression, but I doubt that I would have. The stigma around mental illness had clearly taken up residence in my head, leading me to waste ten years looking for any physical cause to explain my problems. Even a serious diagnosis of a physical illness would have been a relief during those years. IBS and depression were not what I was hoping to hear. I associated therapy closely with mental illness so I suspect I would never have taken that step.

Today I hold the view that therapy should not be reserved only for those who are mentally ill. I found the experience of talking with a totally objective person, someone trained to guide me through the maze of my thoughts, hugely beneficial in learning to understand myself. That self-knowledge is the thing I wouldn't want the genie to take away.

I learned how the experiences in my early life, particularly the period of bullying, had affected the way I approached adult life. If that genie is still offering I would definitely get him to delete the bullying from my back story. Not because it was so hard to survive at the time, but because for years afterwards the hard shell I constructed to protect me from any future attacks became a kind of prison. I developed two separate personas, neither of which was complete. Work Steve was the ambitious perfectionist who never made a mistake, never showed fear or weakness, exuded supreme confidence and did not suffer fools around him. Home Steve was sweet and vulnerable, loving and romantic, fiercely loyal and nurturing. He was the one Anne fell in love with, the one Anne would cuddle as she told him everything was going to be OK. Therapy helped me to reintegrate the two halves again, and to be a whole person in all walks of life.

I have written about the daily use of CBT techniques and self-analysis to manage the negative thoughts. This does take a lot of energy on bad days, but it too brings benefits.

I feel that for a man, particularly one of my generation, I am very in touch with my feelings. I had a period in early retirement when I sought out various men's groups, in an effort to find like-minded men with more progressive attitudes to masculinity. These were men who were at least willing to talk about feelings, which puts them in the minority, but they clearly struggled to identify what those feelings really were. Very often they spoke mainly about who they blamed for their unhappiness – usually a mother or an ex-wife – rather than the root causes of their problems. I suspect they couldn't see these problems, and the format of the groups was such that it was not our place to point them out. We were there to listen and empathise, though I found that difficult in such cases, and ultimately I stopped attending. I also see examples, among friends or family, of adult men who cannot express how they feel nor understand which feelings are driving their behaviour. Depression and therapy have saved me from that blindness.

The daily confrontation of negative thoughts also strips such thoughts of their power to overwhelm me. This means that when something genuinely horrible happens I cope much better than before. The most recent example was losing my father in such a terrible way. I was sad, both during his long illness and at his final passing. Yet I felt I could bear the sadness, and give it space in my head, without it becoming unbearable or feeling the need to repress it. It served me well at his funeral where I gave the eulogy and it serves me well today. I still haven't cried over his death – which I am not convinced is healthy. I find I have to be in extreme anguish before I cry, and the tears come so reluctantly that I don't feel hugely better afterwards. But I credit my mental resilience for not having reached that threshold over Dad. And I credit the tools I use to combat depression for that resilience.

When I started to present the integrated Steve persona in the work context, or socially with close friends, I noticed another significant benefit. People liked me more. I used to kid myself that I did not care what people thought. If they liked me that was fine, but I was not going to compromise my integrity just to be liked. Not surprisingly that version of me was respected in many quarters, and was not without friends, but was not a person you would go to for comfort or reassurance. This cuddlier version of me was however quite approachable, and I discovered I did care. Being liked was nice, and I wanted more. I became a much better manager of teams – not just leading by example as before but by actively supporting the welfare of my team. If I had somehow dodged the bullying episode, or other similar experiences, and the bifurcation this created, maybe I would always have been like this. I will never know. I do know that my depression diagnosis sent me down a path to healing this split and I am grateful for that.

Another benefit came rather late in the day, about eight years before retirement. It only materialised after I was forced by events to tell my employers about my depression, and then chose to tell my work colleagues rather than making some excuse. As I began to realise that I was not being judged negatively for this admission, I became more confident in sharing this information more widely. For years I had feared people would think less of me if they knew, but I had maybe misjudged the times. This was 2009 and a greater openness and acceptance of mental illness was beginning to emerge. Hopefully it has continued to do so since. The worst reaction I had was those who felt awkward talking about it, so would quickly change the subject. Most people were sympathetic and some would start to share their own experiences, maybe of a loved one who suffered but sometimes their own struggles. The more I got these reactions, the more people I told. Then I started to get a new reaction – disbelief.

I don't mean people thought I was lying. I mean that people who had known me, for years in some cases, and thought they had me figured out, couldn't believe that the person they knew was hiding depression. I was clearly very good at it. Even the integrated Steve persona was a pretty confident, outgoing, gregarious person who, even on the bad days, put on his best game face for the outside world. I don't think I did this consciously. It may have been some kind of hangover from the days of fearing to show any weakness. That fear had largely dissipated though so I think it was something else. Some kind of instinct that we all have to show ourselves in the best light to others. Whatever the reason, the first reaction to me talking about my depression was often shock.

One of the non-work activities Anne and I both enjoyed in Luxembourg was called Toastmasters. This is an international organisation, originating in the USA almost a century ago, which promotes public speaking and leadership. I wasn't interested in the leadership bit, I got enough of that during the day, though I was talked into being the President of our club for a while. Clubs which join this organisation arrange evening meetings where people get to work on their public speaking. It is designed to help those who struggle with speaking in public, especially those who suffer with nerves, to improve. Members work their way through a manual of projects, each of which focus on a particular aspect of speaking (e.g. vocal variety) until they grow in confidence and can fluently deliver a 10-minute speech without notes. They have such clubs in the UK too and I recommend them if you also struggle with this useful skill. I was always a confident speaker so I treated the club mainly as an excuse to show off.

Several years into this activity I decided to give a speech on depression. I told the audience that, given the numbers in the room and the incidence of depression in the general population, it was statistically likely that 1.5 people were depressed. So maybe one person was depressed and the other just a little pissed off. I went on to say that I didn't know who the pissed off person was, but the one with depression was me. This was met with more than a few gasps and shocked faces. After my speech, which described some of the aspects of depression covered in this book, several people came up to me. They expressed their disbelief, some said I was very brave, but more importantly that evening, or in the weeks after, a number of our fellow Toastmasters confided in me about their own struggles. Not just people who I thought of as friends either, some people who I thought a bit stand-offish. They said that the fact that "someone like me" had depression made them feel better about themselves.

Over the years more people have expressed a similar view and it planted a seed in my mind which has been germinating ever since. Increasingly we are seeing celebrities open up about their mental health issues. While writing this book, several top international rugby players and a former F1 champion have told of their struggles. This clearly helps people who look up to these stars, and who have issues of their own, overcome the stigma and silence which surround mental health. On a much smaller scale people like me, who project an image of being strong and capable to those around them, can help to reduce that stigma by being open about their illness. So over time I have become a bit of an advocate for telling all – even when the circumstances don't require it.

I help to run a youth club with five youth workers, which serves local teenagers. Amongst both the staff and the kids we help we have neuro-divergent people and people with mental illnesses. I am convinced that they relate better to me because I am open to them about my depression and we can have a chat about the pros and cons of our latest drugs over a coffee. I can also empathise strongly with them when they need a break to recover. This is very rewarding and yet one more thing I would want my genie to leave alone.

I began to wonder if I could help more. Setting an example as someone who appears fine but is open about their depression could go only so far. For those few who ask me advice on how to cope I try to explain what works for me. What if I could reach more people? Would people read a book by a complete unknown who claimed to be a Happy Depressive. There was only one way to find out.

The final upside of depression was that I had plenty I wanted to write about.

Voice 1:	"I think it's time for Anne to have her say."
Voice 2:	"Whoa, hang on there. Are you serious?"
Voice 1:	"Yes, why not?."
Voice 2:	"Well, what is she going to say?"
Voice 1:	"That is up to her."
Voice 2:	"What if she says you are a pain in the arse?"
Voice 1:	"Maybe I am sometimes."
Voice 2:	"No doubt about it."
Voice 1:	"But I think people will be interested in her perspective."
Voice 2:	"OK mate, it's your funeral – or should I say divorce."
Voice 1:	"We have made it this far together. I think we can survive an honest appraisal of life with a depressive. "

14

A View from Her Indoors

I am very fortunate that I have never suffered from depression. I have of course been depressed, anxious and low many times in my life. I have been through hormone hell in the form of premenstrual tension and the menopause, and although this was highly unpleasant at the time it was at least readily attributable to a cause. Basing my approach to loving my happy depressive on my own personal experience of depression sometimes went wrong in the early days, but also I got a few things right, even if it was by accident.

If you are reading this book as the person caring for someone living with depression then I hope my contribution will help you. It may allow you to feel less alone and you might be able to avoid some of my errors as you negotiate the joys and pitfalls of loving a depressive (happy or otherwise).

Let's start with what, for us, became a pivotal moment in Steve addressing his depression - the conversation on the bench on the walk through Purley. I don't remember the specifics of what I said to him that day. The general feeling was that I felt cheated that he was burnt out and withdrawn with me at the weekends but continued to function during the week at work. I was making it an issue about me, or at least our relationship, so I was taking a bit of a risk. Although I felt guilty at the time for raising it I don't regret it. That's because he is an amazing person who recognised the seriousness of what I was saying and had the courage, fortitude and stamina to do something about it.

Before that conversation, and for quite some time afterwards, I would interpret him being depressed as a sign there was something wrong with our relationship, or with me. This stems from my own experience of being depressed, which 99% of the time is attributable to something sad or wrong in my life. The PMS followed the pattern of my menstrual cycle, so hormone hell could be tolerated as I knew the cause. I would therefore look for a reason why he was depressed.

Another factor in play was that I made him happy. Being with me was a positive thing in his life so when he was depressed I subconsciously thought it was my job to cheer him up. Sometimes my insecurities about his feelings for me would kick in when he was low and withdrawn. We had many an argument where he would call me egocentric and tell me "it's not all about you!" I would resent this and get quite angry, because I thought this was unfair, and that he was asking me to ignore my feelings to make life easier for him. I realise now that this is not what he was asking at all. He just needed space and the possibility of going low or to not be present for a while in order to drag himself up again.

So, my first piece of advice is to not look to rescue your loved one, not to try to absorb their depression or look for ways that the depression can be fixed. Depression is a bitch and it can bite you on a lovely sunny day when you are having a good time. I got something really useful from reading Matt Haigh's book about depression (*Reasons to Stay Alive*). His partner would ask "Is there anything practical that I can do to help?" This is such a useful question because often there isn't anything you can do, and that's okay.

It's horrible to see someone you love go down into a negative or lethargic state but "it's not all about you" so I have learned to let him roll with it. However I would advocate some self-care for the lover of a depressive. It's not disloyal or horrible to share your concerns with people outside the relationship. Steve is very astute and empathetic, so he knows sometimes he is hard to live with. One of the things that makes him lower still, when Voice 2 is in full flow, is the impact he's having on me. Sharing your concerns with a friend is essential to your well-being, and knowing you are getting external support can mean one less thing for your depressive to worry about.

Sometimes you might feel conflicted because you love them but you resent the depression. If you are like me this can become a negative loop in your head. Generally withdrawing from the situation is my preferred option and doing something away from him that I enjoy for a personal reset works more often than not. Their depression is bad for us as spectators, but it is worse for them and we can at least get away from them for a bit, whereas they are stuck with themselves.

Don't walk on eggshells around them. Ask them to make a cup of tea and be prepared for the look that indicates you have just asked them to do something they will find really difficult, but still ask and expect them to make that cuppa.

There are also positives to loving someone with depression. You are very important to them. This can be a big source of self-worth but you might also be concerned that you are indirectly benefitting from their condition. They need you so much because you ease their pain – so if they got better would they need you less? Would they love you less?

Steve has developed a really good level of self-awareness, empathy and coping strategies which, when it's my turn to get low, makes him an excellent friend and counsellor. It is also good to be aware of the randomness of depression. As a result the really good days are treasured things to be enjoyed and it helps to take the pressure off on the bad days.

So if your loved one is going down, try not to join them on the journey. Don't try to save them from the dip. Don't try to find a cause or a remedy and take a step back. Share your concerns and frustrations with others if you need to. Relish the good days and be gentle and accept you cannot be the solution on the bad days.

Voice 1: "I think that's it – nothing more to say."

Voice 2: "Thank God for that "

Voice 1: "Maybe I should add a summary section."

Voice 2: "Yeah – then they can skip to that and avoid all that verbiage."

Voice 1: "If they do fair enough. As long as it helps someone I don't care."

Voice 2: "Now he thinks he is Mother Theresa."

Voice 1: "Just a Happy Depressive looking to spread the love."

Voice 2: "I think I am going to be sick."

In a Nutshell

Hopefully you will have reached this chapter after reading all the others and I also hope that by sharing my experiences I have shown why I recommend the things that I do. If you have skipped straight to this chapter, as Voice 2 suggested, then all is forgiven. We are all busy people and sometimes it is nice to get a potted summary when we are feeling under pressure. If you want the detail behind the advice then skip back to the relevant chapter.

When I am dealing with friends or family I usually avoid giving advice. I believe that even when people seem to be coming to you for answers, what they really want is to be heard and to get reassurance that what they have already decided to do makes sense. If they are really stuck I try to get them to outline their options and maybe help them to see ones they may have missed, but the final decision has to be their own.

In a way I am making an exception to this rule by writing this book. Though I aim to be like that friend you can talk to over a cuppa, I don't have the luxury of hearing what you have to say. All I can do is lay out what has worked for me, which perhaps gives you some options you have not considered, and hope that it helps you to decide how you approach living with depression.

If like me you have no clear memories of your childhood then:

a)   Probably shelve those plans for your autobiography
b)   Don't let it put you off therapy altogether

It doesn't necessarily mean that there are dark episodes in your past that you have repressed. You may have simply had a nice but uneventful childhood. If you choose a form of therapy such as psychodynamic counselling, as I did, then the therapist will want to explore those blanks, but you will soon get on to bits you can remember, and these can yield useful information about the way you behave as an adult. If the thought of delving into your past is just too daunting then maybe choose another form of psychotherapy that focusses more on the present and the future. Whilst I can't offer any advice from personal experience, I know from the stories of others that they work for many people.

Start to recognise whether you also have two voices in your head. Learn to separate Voice 2 – the voice of doom and gloom – from Voice 1 – the voice of hope and reason. Accept that Voice 2 is the mouthpiece for your depression and that it is best ignored. It will remind you of all your irrational fears and potentially prevent you from doing things that will prove to be really rewarding, even if they seemed scary before you started. On the bad days when that voice is in full flow, do your best to distract yourself in any way that works.

If you have the misfortune to be bullied at school then try to remember that this will be a short but horrible period and that you will get through it. Though it may feel like it, it is not due to any defect or inadequacy in you. It has much more to do with the insecurities of those who are doing the bullying. Find your own way to get through it, whatever works best for you, remembering that better times are just ahead.

Once you come out the other side of this painful episode intact, be aware of the strategies you used to survive. They may no longer be helpful or healthy, so don't let those bullies win by handicapping yourself through adult life and putting up defences for an attack that will never come.

Wherever you can, seek out a friend, family member or loved one with whom you can be completely yourself, warts and all, without judgement or rejection. Explain your condition to them and help them to help you. Be patient as it takes them time to come to terms with your disease and to accept the times when they are powerless. Be kind and nurture this precious resource, identify the signs that they need support too sometimes and be there for them. Don't push them away when you cannot face the world. Think of them as your safe space where you can do what you need to do to get through the day without putting on your brave face. If you cannot find that safe space in a person, try to craft one for yourself where you can practice self-care.

If you are offered anti-depressant pills to help with your condition do not reject the offer out of fear or shame. They can help to slow down those negative thoughts to the point where your other strategies have a chance of working. If the first drug doesn't work or has side effects that you cannot bear then try another or even a few more. Be assertive with the doctors and see if you can find the sweet spot in your medication. If it becomes less effective over time modify your dose or try something new. The aim is for those bad days to be outnumbered by the good ones, so that the run of bad days is always short.

If you are unlucky enough to have depression which is resistant to drugs, or if the side effects of everything you have tried have proved unbearable, clearly you need to find alternatives to the drugs. I have no personal experience to offer in this area, with the possible exception of hypnotherapy which did prove good for relaxing an anxious mind. The aim is to simulate that effect of slowing down the flow of negative thoughts to the point where the energy needed to deal with them is within your capacity.

It is likely you will be offered CBT, so give it a try as it really worked for me. If it proves too cold and logical for your temperament try newer techniques with similar aims. If you can master these skills then in time you will be able to intercept the negative messages Voice 2 is spouting at the speed of thought and rob them of their power, so that Voice 1 starts to win. When it works it is a useful technique but may not be enough on its own.

If the negative thoughts seem too powerful then consider psychotherapy to cut them off at source. It can be surprising how much of the emotion attached to these thoughts is not due to the current events that appear to generate the reaction, but to past experiences which were much more traumatic. Learn to separate the two and to develop reactions more appropriate to what is happening in the here and now.

Once you have assembled all your tools to fight this disease (preferably before you reach your forties but even then there is plenty of life left to live) then develop the coping strategy that works best for you. Decide how much of a concession you need or want to make to your depression and how much you think you can achieve with the energy it leaves you. You may not decide, as I did, to fight through even the bad days to get to work and pursue the type of career you wish to follow. If you do then the concept of the early morning all systems check may appeal.

Once you have assessed whether you are facing an amazing, good, poor or bad day then moderate your targets for that day accordingly. On the amazing and good days still remember to pace yourself so that you don't get exhausted and take a nosedive. On the poor days the distractions of work and life and interacting with other people may get you through. If not, have as much of a play-day as your job allows and know you can make up the slack another day. On the bad days do as little as possible and rest as soon as you can. If external factors push you into overdoing it then take a break and let yourself recover.

If you are retired then don't assume that all the triggers for your depression will disappear and acknowledge that this is one of the biggest changes in your life. It is going to take time to find a new way of being you, and you are going to need modified coping strategies to help you through. Make the most of the new freedom to rest whenever you need it and treasure the fact that the external pressure to perform has gone. Keep the all-systems check and plan your day accordingly.

It does not hurt to focus from time to time on all the positives in your life and count your blessings. This can help to make the downtimes easier to accept. Many people face difficult situations in their life that make it so much harder to work their way out of the depression. If like me you are privileged in many ways acknowledge your advantages and show empathy to those who are less fortunate. Don't fall into the trap of feeling guilty for being depressed despite your large dose of luck. People who are discriminated against face a much bigger risk of depression, but depression itself does not discriminate. It can strike anyone and it is not your fault that it picked on you.

When the fact that your depression is hanging around is getting you down, try to remember the upsides it also brings. The techniques and strategies needed to combat the illness can bring you to a level of self-knowledge many do not achieve. You will be more in touch with your feelings and better at spotting the signs of distress in others. If you succeed in shedding the stigma around your condition, and can be open about it to others, you will help them open up too, and can maybe act as a role model for how to cope. Showing your vulnerability in the right circumstances can make you seem much more human and approachable to others, and make you easier to like. It's OK to enjoy being liked.

Anne would tell you not to try to rescue the depressive you live with and also not to take on responsibility for their happiness. You will be so important to them and they will need you a lot at times, but at other times it is best to just take a step away and care for yourself too. Let them go down when they have no choice, but don't go down with them, just enjoy the cuddle when they come back up.

So that's it. Whether you have read four pages, the whole book or somewhere in between I hope that you have found the book easy to understand and helpful to you in some small way. If you did then I am an even Happier Depressive.

About the Author

Steve Richards was born and raised in South Wales. He never learned Welsh but was imbued with the Welsh love of language from an early age. At school he was torn between his love of English, literature and storytelling and his aptitude for mathematics and physics which seemed to offer more obvious career paths. He chose the latter and enjoyed an interesting professional life, firstly as a civil engineer working on major transport projects and later as a technical advisor to the European Investment Bank in Luxembourg. Throughout his working years he tried hard to keep his creative side alive, using the small gaps a busy career offers to write short stories and articles on subjects close to his heart. He also pursued private study of psychology and on retirement took the masters level course in Psychology he had always dreamed of completing. In retirement he spends most of his time on voluntary work with young people, particularly disadvantaged teenagers: working with boys to encourage alternative and positive models of masculinity; working in schools to improve sex and relationship education; and with young offenders undertaking community service. He is married to Anne who helps him cope with life and has the dubious honour of being the first to read everything he writes. He is not a professional counsellor or therapist but offers something which those professionals may lack – lived experience. He has suffered from depression since his late twenties but has lived a fulfilling and happy life and hopes to do so for many years to come.

Did you find The Happy Depressive useful to you, or at least interesting? Do you have your own coping mechanisms and strategies that you would like to share? If so I would love to get your reactions to the book. If you would like to you can post feedback at www.happydepressive.com.

Milton Keynes UK
Ingram Content Group UK Ltd.
UKHW010727150524
442746UK00001B/7